Runs, Hits, and an Era

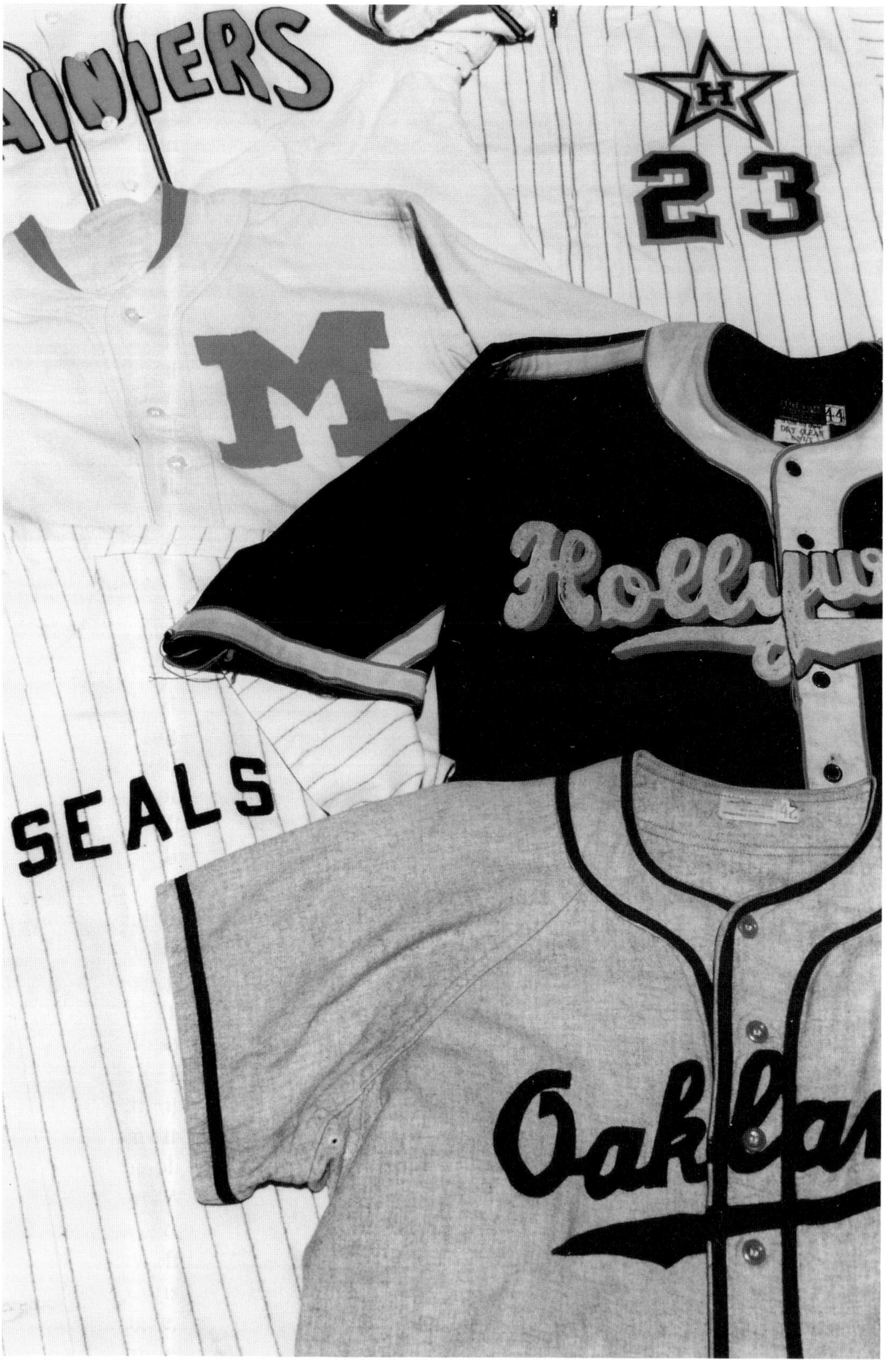
H
23
M
SEALS

Runs, Hits, and an Era

The Pacific Coast League, 1903–58

Paul J. Zingg

Mark D. Medeiros

Published for the Oakland Museum

by the University of Illinois Press

Urbana and Chicago

This book is printed on acid-free paper.

Frontispiece photograph by Doug McWilliams.
The Oakland Museum Collection.

Library of Congress Cataloging-in-Publication Data

Zingg, Paul J., 1947–
    Runs, hits, and an era : the Pacific Coast League, 1903–58 / Paul
J. Zingg, Mark D. Medeiros
        p.   cm.
    Includes bibliographical references and index.
    ISBN 0-252-02117-7 (cloth). — ISBN 0-252-06402-X (paper).
    1. Pacific Coast League—History. 2. Baseball—California—
History. I. Medeiros, Mark D. II. Title.
GV875.P33Z56   1994
796.357'64'09794—dc20   93-47408
                                                                CIP

Contents

Preface

The power of a baseball cap. Having always had a passion for baseball history and being a native Californian, I traced my baseball roots to an interest in the Pacific Coast League (PCL). Since the 1903–58 glory days of the PCL preceded my birth, though, I took to the written word for my understanding of the league. Not an easy feat, but what I digested piqued my interest. Joe DiMaggio, Jigger Statz, Lefty O'Doul, Ted Williams, Steve Bilko, and Billy Martin—did these guys really play in the PCL?! From the early Portland teams to the 1934 Los Angles Angels and the dominant Seattle teams of the 1940s, it was clear that PCL talent was extraordinary and the caliber of play was high. Steeped in statistics, championships, and stars, I thought I had a solid understanding of the league. But I was as mistaken as a hanging curveball to Luke Easter.

My real PCL education came after I purchased a 1950 Oakland Oaks replica baseball cap, a wardrobe decision I did not make lightly. Proudly donning my new headgear, I set off for the Oakland Coliseum to watch the A's play their modern version of the game. My Oaks cap paid an immediate dividend when a stranger walking past a tailgate party I was attending noticed my cap and stopped to share his PCL stories. He spoke with the excitement and fondness of a grandfather discussing his favorite grandchild's first steps. Later in the day, a woman standing ahead of me in the concession line commented on my cap and shared with me how, as a single mother, she and her two sons had become fans of the Sacramento Solons. One of the Solons, it seems, lived in her neighborhood and took the time to teach her sons how to throw a curveball and even how to change the oil in the family car. Both these encounters whetted my appetite for a true PCL education.

An annual pilgrimage for the past two years to the PCL Historical Society meeting, a labor of love headed by Dick Beverage, continued my education. The meeting brings together fans and players for a day of shooting the breeze, sharing memorabilia and stories, and recapturing the PCL magic. Hosting a luncheon at the Oakland Museum for former players and fans and attending various Coast League reunions reinforced in my mind the closeness among players, fans, and the PCL cities in which franchises were located. Seeing the care and spirit of collectors such as Dick Dobbins and Bob Reiss warmed my heart. The search for my baseball roots turned out golden!

Given the number of transplants to California and the West Coast, not to mention the time that has passed since the PCL glory years, many fans (an estimated 12 million annually attend major league games on the West Coast) know very little about their baseball heritage and therefore don't understand the importance to the game of the Pacific Coast League. Baseball fans in other parts of the country probably know even less about a league that once rivaled the National and American leagues for player talent and excitement. The Oakland Museum, by mounting an exhibit and cooperating with the University of Illinois Press in the publication of *Runs, Hits, and an Era: The Pacific Coast League, 1903–58,* is doing its part to fill the void. Sure, PCL teams played high-caliber baseball, but there was more to it than that. Labor relations, race relations, technological advances, West Coast history, civic pride, players in short pants, and intimate ballparks—that's also what the PCL was about. So slap on your favorite baseball cap and sit back and enjoy the story that follows.

—Mark D. Medeiros

Acknowledgments

A gracious thank you must go to the Oakland Museum's chief curator of history (and Sacramento Solon fan) L. Thomas Frye. His belief in the project, his strong support, and his knowing exactly when to lend a hand were extremely valuable in putting together a project of this magnitude. It doesn't hurt that he also knows just about everybody on the West Coast.

The dynamic duo of Marcia Eymann and Cherie Newell displayed tireless energy throughout the project. Marcia's sports history background includes an exhibition on the history of boxing. Her research brought exciting photographs to this book and the related exhibition. Her people skills are outstanding, and as exhibition coordinator she has done everything I asked and more. Cherie, the assistant project director, was a quick study on the subject of baseball and handled all aspects of her job with the grace of Artie Wilson fielding a grounder.

Paul J. Zingg, formerly dean of liberal arts at Saint Mary's College and currently dean of the College of Liberal Arts at California Polytechnic State University in San Luis Obispo, wrote the main essay. Straight from an outstanding publication entitled *Harry Hooper: An American Baseball Life,* Paul handled his assignment with the smooth style of a Joe DiMaggio stroke and the scholarly manner the Pacific Coast League deserves.

When I say we could not have put together the exhibit without Dick Dobbins I am speaking literally. His passion for the PCL drove him to develop the ultimate collection of PCL memorabilia. His knowledge of Bay Area baseball is expansive, and we should all look forward to his book on the subject.

Also helping to keep the PCL spirit alive is Richard Beverage, author of two PCL team histories—on the Los Angeles Angels and the Hollywood Stars. Dick is president of the PCL Historical Society and warmly welcomed me into the group.

Thank you also to Phil Mumma, Jessica Statz, Helen Hannah Campbell, Denis Cavagnero, Jules Tygiel, John Spalding, Don Solem, and many others who shared their PCL experiences with me.

A very special thank you to the California Council for the Humanities, the Walter and Elise Haas Foundation, the Oakland Museum Women's Board, Chevron, the Oakland Athletics, and the San Francisco Giants for generously funding the exhibit.

—Mark D. Medeiros

Runs, Hits, and an Era

THE INDEPENDENT GOLD HUNTER ON HIS WAY TO CALIFORNIA

Aside from the ubiquitous pick and shovel, this well-equipped forty-niner carried an assortment of cooking pots, sausages, whiskey, gold scales, and a battery of weapons. ("The Independent Gold Hunter on His Way to California," lithograph by Kellog & Comstock, New York and Hartford; printed by Ensign & Taylor, Buffalo, ca. 1850. The Oakland Museum Collection.)

1

The Nineteenth-Century Game

More than hopes and dreams filled the air of San Francisco in the early days of the Gold Rush. Especially on Sunday afternoons, despite blue laws that restricted recreational activities on the Sabbath, a tightly wrapped, leather covered rag ball occasionally flew high above the city plazas as "full grown persons engaged very industriously in the game known as town ball."[1] This element of the transplanted urban culture of the eastern tradesmen and mechanics who had crossed a continent to California had no practical bearing on their pursuit of happiness in the new Eldorado. But like their numbers, which had already transformed San Francisco from a tiny hamlet of about one thousand inhabitants in 1848 to a city of almost thirty-five thousand just four years later, the fortune-seekers brought with them new recreational interests, the populace necessary to sustain them, and one game, in particular, that would profoundly affect the Bay Area and the western sporting scene ever after.

On the New York and New Jersey playing fields, townball had already evolved into baseball by 1850, and the appeal of the game had encouraged the formation of several clubs and the start of competition among them. On the eve of the Civil War, over seventy clubs existed in Brooklyn alone, and the games among them had begun to serve as occasions for neighborhood boosterism and civic pride. Spectator interest in the interclub contests quickly extended to sectional rivalries as well. The rivalry between Brooklyn and New York City became particularly intense, reflecting the political and cultural differences of the two most populous cities in the country (at the time), separated only by the East River. Presaging the importance of the intrastate and local rivalries in the California and West Coast baseball leagues, the *Brooklyn Eagle* proclaimed in 1867 that "nowhere has the National game of Baseball taken a firmer hold than in Brooklyn and nowhere are there better players." Victories over nearby rivals were especially sweet. "If we are ahead of the big city in nothing else," the *Eagle* observed, "we can beat her in baseball."[2]

Veterans of these eastern diamonds pioneered in bringing the game to the Pacific Coast. San Francisco's first organized team, the Eagle Base Ball Club, which traced its roots to 1859, counted among its founding members John Fisher, who had played ball with the Empires of New York.[3] Similarly, William and James Shephard, brothers who had competed for the New York Knickerbockers at Hoboken's Elysian Fields, helped establish the Pacific Base Ball Club in 1862. Waller Wallace, a former member of the Brooklyn Peconics, founded, managed, and pitched for the California Theater Baseball Club around the same time.[4]

Although competition among these and other Bay Area teams occurred sporadically during the Civil War years, baseball on the West Coast, as throughout the country, awaited the restoration of peace before its full indulgence. After Appomattox, a virtual mania took hold of the sport. Veterans of both armies returned home with a real enthusiasm for the game they had played in their encampments, and they set about organizing their own ball clubs. By the end of the decade, *Wilkes' Spirit of the Times,* the leading sporting publication of the era, estimated that nearly two thousand baseball clubs existed throughout the nation.[5]

The Bay Area contributed over twenty-five clubs to this total, several of which organized themselves in 1866 as the Pacific Base Ball Convention. Promoting "championship" matches and offering a "splendid ball bat elaborately mounted in silver" to the region's best team, the convention drew sizable crowds to its games, especially those played at the Recreation Grounds at the corner of Twenty-fifth and Folsom streets in south San Francisco near Potrero Hill.[6] Play began there, at the West Coast's first enclosed baseball field, on Thanksgiving Day 1868, when over three thousand spectators watched the Eagle Club stake an initial claim to Bay Area baseball bragging rights with a 37-23 win over the Wide Awakes of Oakland.

Seeking to promote the popularity of baseball, the convention invited the Cincinnati Red Stockings to play a series of games against its teams in the fall of 1869. The completion of the transcontinental railroad in May made such an invitation possible, and, when the Red Stockings accepted, the Bay Area baseball fraternity reacted with joy and optimism about the outcome of the contests. The eastern visitors, however, were no ordinary opponent. Nearing the end of a nationwide tour that carried them almost twelve thousand miles and attracted over two hundred thousand spectators to their games, the Red Stockings were a powerful contingent of skilled professionals who impressed spectators and the media with their prowess and physiques (a reporter for the San Francisco *Chronicle* particularly admired their "well-formed calves").[7] Like every team that faced the Red Stockings that year, the Californians were no match for Harry Wright's boys, who dispatched them by a combined score of 289-22 in five games.[8]

The thrashing at the hands of the Cincinnati nine had an understandably discouraging effect on baseball enthusiasts in the Bay Area, and at-

The meeting of the rails at Promontory Point, Utah, in May 1869. With the completion of the transcontinental railroad, professional East Coast baseball teams could compete on the West Coast. (Photograph by Andrew J. Russell. The Oakland Museum Collection.)

tendance at games began to fall off. By June 1870, though, the press noted "new life" in West Coast baseball, and the Pacific Convention played an active role in encouraging the formation of new clubs.[9] Over the next few years, teams formed not only in such established baseball towns as Oakland, Berkeley, Alameda, Stockton, and Sacramento but in communities throughout the state, from Humboldt County to San Diego.

On its most fundamental level in these far-flung locales, the game provided enjoyment for player and spectator alike, if not skillful play on the field. Yet the absence of high-caliber play neither dampened fervor for the game nor precluded the development of intense local rivalries. Fierce competition between the Siskiyou Mountaineers of Ft. Jones and the Eureka Actives in California's northern counties, the Johnsville and Portola clubs in the gold country above Lake Tahoe, and the Santa Cruz

The powerful, highly skilled 1869 Cincinnati Red Stockings were the first professional East Coast team to play on the West Coast. (National Baseball Library and Archive, Cooperstown, N.Y.)

Runs,

Hits,

and

an Era

Manager-outfielder Harry Wright of the Cincinnati Red Stockings, ca. 1869. (National Baseball Library and Archive, Cooperstown, N.Y.)

Olympics and Watsonville Occidentals on the central coast underscored the dramatic expansion and appeal of the game. Not content for supremacy on the local diamonds, small-town nines occasionally ventured forth to take on the veteran clubs of San Francisco. On November 17, 1878, for example, the Intrepids of Marysville, billing themselves as "the champions of Northern California," challenged the Eagle Club. The visitors could not handle the curve balls of the Eagles' professional pitcher, however, and fell 10-0 before two thousand spectators.[10]

As the status of the Eagles' pitcher suggested, West Coast clubs had imitated the behavior of their eastern counterparts and abandoned a strictly amateur commitment to the game. The establishment of the National Association of Professional Base Ball Players in March 1871 had confirmed a direction for the game that the Brooklyn and New York clubs had initiated when they provided sub-rosa payments to such players as James Creighton, Joe Start, and Dickie Pearce in the early 1860s. The superior play of the all-salaried Red Stockings particularly convinced Bay Area clubs, as it had the largely amateur nines the Cincinnati team defeated in the East, that competitive success depended on a fuller development of the skills of the game than what could be achieved in approaching baseball as simply a casual recreation. The example of the Red Stockings democratized the field of play, bringing blue-collar workers to rosters that had previously been dominated by middle-class men seeking only wholesome diversion. And in doing so it transformed the character of competition.

The mixture of amateurs and semiprofessionals on the baseball diamonds of the West Coast reflected the debate elsewhere in the country regarding the purpose of play, but it deterred neither the movement toward professionalization nor popular appreciation for the brand of play that resulted. By 1876, the men of the Pacific Base Ball Convention, buoyed by the expansion of the game and confident in the quality of its ballplayers, were anxious once again to test their skills against outside competition. The occasion this time was the nation's centennial celebration, and fifteen Bay Area players, calling themselves the Centennials to mark as well the one hundredth anniversary of the founding of San Francisco, set out across the country to compete in a baseball tournament in Philadelphia. Led by Delos Ashley, a pitcher who specialized in swift "in and out shoots," and catcher Thomas "Brick" Cullen, the Californians won six of seven games over the eleven days of the tournament.[11]

Although the Centennials' performance underscored the quality of the homegrown talent in the Bay Area and momentarily checked any interest in importing expensive players from other areas of the country, the example of the Red Stockings, a team that fielded only one Cincinnati native, was not completely lost. The bottom line in the increasingly competitive West Coast baseball world, as elsewhere, was winning, and if that could not be accomplished with a team of local heroes, then the importation of professionals to wear the club colors was recognized as a justifiable and appropriate step to take. It was perhaps fitting that a former member of the Red Stockings, Cal McVey, should play a key role in this development in the Bay Area. Moving to Oakland in 1879, McVey organized the Bay City Base Ball Club and quickly established it as one of the best in the area. His players demonstrated their prowess in convincing fashion by beating Cap Anson's touring Chicago White Sox, the National League champions of 1880, four games to two in a postseason series.

But McVey and others like him were an expensive and often unreliable investment. When McVey left baseball within a couple of years of his arrival in Oakland to become superintendent of an irrigation company in Hanford, California, his club collapsed. James "Pud" Galvin, who would go on to record 361 wins in a pitching career with Buffalo and Pittsburgh, was offered $2,000 by the San Francisco Athletics for the 1880 season, but he hung around for only a month before bigger money lured him back east. Players like Edward "The Only" Nolan and William "Bald Billie" Barnie were barely around long enough for Bay Area fans to appreciate their nicknames before resuming their professional careers with eastern teams. Increasingly, the Bay Area clubs returned to the practice of recruiting local talent for their rosters.

In January 1878, four San Francisco clubs—the Eagles, the Renos, the Californias, and the Athletics—founded the West Coast's first baseball league, the Pacific Base Ball League (PBBL), to showcase local talent. Within a year, the California League (CL), a second four-team circuit including a nine from Oakland, emerged to satisfy the growing baseball appetite and attract the increasing entertainment dollar of Bay Area fans. By 1882, however, the California League had folded and the PBBL was barely surviving. Their problems paralleled those affecting the game in the East, where the inattention and ineptitude of club owners and league officials, such as there were, and less predictable factors as a downturn in local economies or the decimation of team rosters through the defection of players to other clubs, had seen teams—and entire leagues—collapse even before seasons had ended. As late as 1897, in fact, only ten of seventeen professional leagues that started the season actually completed it.[12]

Recognizing the need for a new approach to organize and manage the professional game more effectively and profitably, William Ambrose Hulbert, a charter stockholder and president of the Chicago White Stockings Club of the National Association of Professional Base Ball Players (NAPBBP), assembled the representatives of several eastern and midwestern clubs in a New York hotel room in February 1876. Fully tuned to the business gospel of the era that preached consolidation and control, the group arbitrarily moved to exclude the players on their clubs from any

Cal McVey, former first baseman and manager for the Cincinnati Red Stockings, moved to Oakland in 1879 and organized the Bay City Base Ball Club. Photograph ca. 1875. (National Baseball Library and Archive, Cooperstown, N.Y.)

management authority and reconstituted their sport as an owner-labor arrangement. They called their new organization the National League of Professional Base Ball Clubs. Within a year, the National League had established understandings with two other circuits, the International Association and the League Alliance, that respected the territorial rights and player contracts of all parties. The compact provided the basic framework for the landmark National Agreement of 1883 among the National League, American Association, and Northwestern League—an agreement that strengthened the owners' control over their clubs and drew a distinction between "major" and "minor" status for the professional leagues.

The launching of the National Agreement came on the eve of a period of economic prosperity and urban growth throughout the country that contributed to the agreement's success. Baseball people on the West Coast appreciated both the example of the National Agreement and the opportunity for expanding economic and population bases to reform the structure and conduct of their game. Like developments on the East Coast, these efforts depended on the leadership of key individuals. No one was more important in this regard than John J. "Major" Mone. Elected president of a revived California League in 1882 at age thirty-three, the San Francisco attorney and commissioner of the city's superior court focused his attention on strengthening the integrity of the game and building greater public trust in it.[13] During his eleven years as president of the CL, Mone helped codify the rules of play on the field along the lines of the National League and introduced numerous measures to drive ruffianism out of the game.

His efforts in both regards reflected the broad attempt nationally of owners, publicists, and entrepreneurs in other aspects of the baseball business to clean up their product and market its appeal around a set of traditional middle-class values. This was no small challenge for a sporting world that Henry Chadwick, editor of *The Spalding Guide,* described as contaminated by the twin evils of "the saloon and the brothel."[14] His boss, Albert G. Spalding, even suggested that ballplayers were probably best kept in cages between games. By introducing rules to prohibit the sale of liquor to ballplayers at games, to forbid their smoking cigars or cigarettes on the field of play, to curb vulgar language, and, perhaps most important, to ban betting at the ballparks, Major Mone and others like him aimed for a code of player conduct that would improve the quality of play and earn "the confidence and support of the refined and cultured classes of American citizenship."[15]

Notwithstanding the occasional gunshots fired into the air by the partisans of one team or the other who hoped to distract the fielding efforts of their opponents, or the persistent charges of immorality levied against the Sabbath-breaking ballplayers (many having adopted pseudonyms to escape the wrath of their parents), the California League had achieved sufficient respectability and stability by the late 1880s to expand its operations. The league roster for the 1886 season, for example, included for the first time a team outside the immediate Bay Area—the Altas of Sacramento—and CL facilities improved significantly as owners sought to provide patrons of the game with more attractive and comfortable viewing environs. The Alameda Grounds, home to the Oakland Greenhood and Moran club, boasted cushioned seats for its spectators, while the Haight Street Grounds at the eastern end of Golden Gate Park in San Francisco featured private boxes and carriage drivers for the city's social elite, including Charles Crocker of the Central Pacific Railroad, M. H. De Young, publisher of the San Francisco *Chronicle,* and members of the Bohemian Club. Women increasingly attended the league's games, encouraged by the inauguration of Ladies Day on May 21, 1886, and the designation of a special seating pavilion for them.

This ca. 1884 photograph is perhaps the earliest of the amateur Greenhood and Moran baseball team. Pictured from left to right are: (top row) manager Tom Robinson, Jack Donovan, W. W.(?) McCurdy, James T. Moran, Harry Nolan, Darby Robinson, Jacob Greenhood; (middle row) Charles Hanna, George Van Haltren, Al Edwards; (bottom row) mascot Charles Van Haltren, Dave Grant and Danny Long. (Photograph courtesy of Bill E. Weiss, from Spaulding, *Always on Sunday.*)

The California League measured its success in the late 1880s and early 1890s in several ways. Its championship season grew from about 30 games in 1886 (San Francisco's Haverly Club topped the league with an 18-11 record) to over 170 games in 1892, reflecting the mild climate in the state, which facilitated play on virtually a year-round basis, and the enormous popularity of the game. The ever-stretching season also meant that players could no longer approach the game as simply an activity for weekends and holidays. More than ever, professional baseball in the West Coast's premier league required the full-time commitment of its players and improved salaries to hold their employment. In 1889, for example, Stockton paid its ace pitcher, Norm Baker, $275 a month, making him the highest paid player in the league (at a time when semiskilled laborers earned less than $500 a year). Overall, though, individual salaries were considerably less than that as monthly payrolls for teams in the CL averaged just under $1,500. A four-team circuit calling itself the Pacific Coast League had promised high wages and opened amid much hoopla in the spring of 1886, but it failed to attract any of the top players from the California League and folded within a few months.

Perhaps the most important mark of the California League's success was the attention it increasingly received from the eastern major leagues. Initially, this interest focused on the first-rate players who emerged from the CL. Beginning in 1881 with Jeremiah Dennis Eldridge, a former student at Saint Mary's College in Oakland who had played professionally as "Jerry Denny" while still a collegian, the California League provided a steady flow of players to the eastern rosters. Following close on Eldridge's heels were Bob Blakiston, Andy Piercy, and three fellow Saint Mary's alumni, Jim Fogarty, Charlie Gaggus, and Joe Corbett, the latter the younger brother of the heavyweight boxing champion "Gentleman" Jim Corbett. Two of the first Hispanic players to reach the major leagues, Vincent Nava and Mike Depangher, hailed from the Bay Area. Ed Morris, a left-handed power pitcher who averaged over three hundred strikeouts a season for Columbus and Pittsburgh from 1884 to 1886, honed his skills in the CL before joining the American Association. Both Oakland's George Van Haltren and San Francisco's Bill "Little Eva" Lange compiled lifetime batting averages of .316 and .330, respectively, in the National League before returning to California. Van Haltren capped his seventeen years in the eastern leagues (1887–1903), with six more in the Pacific Coast League. Lange only played seven seasons with Chicago in the 1890s but compiled such an outstanding record that he was the measure of all players coming from the Pacific Coast for many years. His heroics included a game-saving (but disputed) catch made after crashing through a wooden fence.

Perhaps the most controversial West Coast player before the turn of the century was Charlie Sweeney.[16] As talented on the mound as he was intemperate with the bottle, the former teenage sensation of the San

George Van Haltren, whose career began in the late 1880s with the Greenhood and Moran team, played in the National League for seventeen years before joining the Pacific Coast League in 1904. He returned to his hometown of Oakland to pitch and manage the Oaks from 1905 to 1909. (Photograph by Moses Cohen. The Oakland Museum Collection.)

Francisco Niantics spent a few mercurial seasons in the National League with Providence and St. Louis in the mid-1880s. When Sweeney was sober, he was often brilliant. He won forty-one games during the 1884 season, including a nineteen-strikeout victory over Boston on June 7 that stood as the single-game mark until Roger Clemens of the Red Sox mowed down twenty Seattle Mariners in 1986. When Sweeney was drunk, however, he made a different kind of headline. In April 1894 he killed a man in a barroom brawl and subsequently spent seven years in San Quentin for manslaughter.

Good players were not traveling in just one direction, from west to east. Outside the constraints of the National Agreement, the teams of the California League frequently raided the rosters of the eastern clubs and attracted players who were eager to jump leagues for better pay and improved playing conditions. Reflecting the uneasiness this practice caused the eastern owners, Walter Wallace of *The Sporting Life* observed that "the California League needs looking after" and advised that "no strong efforts should be spared to make the league an ally instead of a menace to national agreement interests."[17] For their part, Mone and the CL magnates similarly recognized that their league's "outlaw" status could work against them. Nothing prohibited the eastern leagues from employing the same tactics to strengthen their lineups. Willing to trade its independence for greater stability in personnel matters, the league agreed to the terms of the National Agreement prior to the start of the 1890 season.

If the proponents of the California League thought that its new status within the fold of organized baseball would ensure security and prosperity, they were sadly disappointed. Attempts to expand the league to San Jose and Los Angeles and to merge with the fledgling Pacific Northwest League (PNL), which included representatives from Tacoma, Seattle, and Portland, overreached the league's resources and threatened the tenuous unity of its members. The former decision brought teams into the CL from more distant locations and smaller population bases, a combination of factors that promised higher operating expenses without reciprocal increases in revenues. The proposed alliance with the PNL collapsed when that league failed in 1892.

With a nationwide economic recession in the early 1890s contributing to hard times for all of organized baseball, an expansionist agenda for West Coast baseball was ill conceived and badly timed. The American Association had already folded after the 1891 season, and the Players' League had collapsed the year before after just one season. Moreover, the $800 that the California League management had expended to accept the terms of the National Agreement and its promise of protection against roster raiding failed to halt the practice. Not content to suffer in silence while other leagues lured their players away, the CL owners retaliated in kind. Bitter salary disputes ensued, further straining club finances and adding to the instability of the entire circuit. Halfway through the 1893 campaign, the league suspended operations.

OLD JUDGE CIGARETTES Goodwin & Co., New York.

Teenage pitching sensation Charlie Sweeney of the California League's San Francisco Niantics went on to a brilliant career with the National League in St. Louis until a drunken brawl and a manslaughter conviction sent him to San Quentin prison in 1894. (National Baseball Library and Archive, Cooperstown, N.Y.)

This 1903 photograph of the Phoenix baseball team from Saint Mary's College features from left to right: (top row) Fred Fergusen, George Bigley, Brother Agnon, J. Callaghan; (middle row) John Devine, John Flynn, professor and coach Tom Phelan, George Poultney, John Rooney; (front row) Fred Fay, Eddie Burns, George Haley. (Collections of Saint Mary's College Archives.)

Baseball on the West Coast suddenly found itself returned to the informal and semiprofessional conditions of the early 1880s. Collegiate nines in the Bay Area, especially those at Saint Mary's and Santa Clara, and athletic clubs throughout the Pacific states satisfied some of the craving for the game, and prize tournaments occasionally revived notions of a regular league. But a sluggish economy and uncertainties about the baseball business in general frustrated any serious attempts to reorganize the California League or something like it for several years.

Finally, in April 1898 two play-for-pay leagues of six teams each—the

Pacific States League and a new California League—began championship seasons, but the poor quality of play and the distractions of the Spanish-American War frustrated their success. Barely a month into their schedules, representatives of the clubs agreed to combine their efforts and reorganize as a single eight-team circuit. Including members beyond the central Bay Area, such as the Santa Cruz Beachcombers, San Jose Prune Pickers, and Fresno Tigers, the new league resurrected the name of the failed circuit of 1886—the Pacific Coast League—and undertook a weekends-only schedule. The league managed to complete its season and even crowned a champion—the Sacramento Gilt Edge—but weak franchises and fan indifference with the amateurish play and shabby administration raised serious doubts about its continuation.

The new league brought more than colorful team names to the West Coast baseball scene, however. It also engaged knowledgeable baseball people who had clear ideas of what it would take to strengthen the professional game. San Francisco attorney Eugene Bert, former Haverly manager Henry Harris, and James T. Moran and J. Cal Ewing of Oakland—the former sponsored the Greenhood and Moran club of the 1880s with his clothing store partner Jacob Greenhood; the latter was the young owner of the PCL's Oakland franchise—particularly appreciated the need to elevate the quality of play on the field. They had a simple formula to achieve this: restrict the number of teams in the league in order to concentrate player talent, protect rosters through abiding to the terms of the National Agreement, and place all players on salary contract. A leaner league of six teams, once again calling itself the California League, opened play on March 26, 1899.

Although the new league experienced some of the problems of its predecessors, namely, imbalance among the teams and poor fan support in the rural towns of San Jose and Watsonville, the overall quality of play improved significantly and the game began to compete seriously again for California's sporting entertainment dollar. Fine-tuning their product even further, league officials trimmed the circuit to four teams in 1900, all in the proven baseball cities of San Francisco, Oakland, Sacramento, and Stockton. The Gilt Edge won a third consecutive pennant, largely on the strong right arm of Jay Hughes, who had won twenty-eight games with Brooklyn the previous year but decided to pitch for his hometown team when the Superbas failed to meet his salary expectations. "Base Ball in California has reached a popularity unknown in fully ten years," reported the San Francisco *Chronicle* as the CL magnates considered another foray into the southern part of the state.[18]

Dropping Stockton from its roster, the California League continued to field a four-team slate when it added a club from Los Angeles for the next two seasons. With a population now exceeding one hundred thousand, Los Angeles trailed only San Francisco in size on the West Coast; it also offered much sounder prospects for success as a professional base-

The Sacramento Gilt Edge team, owned and managed by Edward Kripp, garnered three California League championships in the 1890s. The man pictured on the far right is believed to be Kripp, ca. 1887. (Sacramento Archives and Museum Collection Center.)

ball city in 1901 than it had in 1893, its last year in the league. The Angels were victorious at the turnstiles and on the field. Also nicknamed the "Looloos" because their playing field, Chutes Park, sat adjacent to an amusement park that featured an elaborate chute slide, the club regularly played to overflow crowds in its five-thousand-seat home. Led by Ed Householder's .300 hitting and Oscar Jones's twenty-nine pitching victories in 1901 and thirty-six in 1902, Los Angeles averaged eighty-six wins in the two campaigns but finished second each time.

Finding renewed credibility with the press and public for both the quality of its product on the field and the effective management of its affairs, California League officials and owners looked to strengthen their hold on the West Coast baseball market. Two new directions, though employing old strategies, seemed imminent for the CL at the close of the 1902 season. The successful renewal of a league franchise in southern California suggested that expansion northward would pay off as well. The league again eyed the Pacific Northwest, where the Pacific National League, comprised of teams from Portland, Seattle, Tacoma, Butte, and Helena, was in its second season of play. The California League also considered returning to the fold of organized baseball, a status that it had not enjoyed since 1899, the last year it paid its National Agreement dues. In September 1901, frustrated with the raging war between the National League and Ban Johnson's upstart American League, the heads of seven minor leagues formed their own National Association to protect their interests. The California League did not join the new association immediately, preferring to operate as an outlaw while it awaited resolution of the eastern baseball situation. The league's eventual response to the issues of expansion and incorporation radically affected not only its organization but the entire structure of professional baseball on the West Coast.

Notes

1. *Daily Alta California,* Jan. 14, 1852, 2.
2. Quoted in Adelman, *A Sporting Time,* 132.
3. Lange, *History of Baseball,* 6–7; Nemec, "Baseball in the San Francisco Bay Area," 3; and San Francisco *Morning Call,* Apr. 7, 1890, which provided biographical sketches "of the men who have aided in bringing the national sport to its present prosperous condition" in San Francisco.
4. Lange, *History of Baseball,* 6–7.
5. *Wilkes' Spirit of the Times,* Sept. 26, 1869.
6. Issel and Cherney, *San Francisco,* 65.
7. San Francisco *Chronicle,* Sept. 26, 1869.
8. Accounts of the Red Stockings' 1869 season and tour include Barney, "Of Rails and Red Stockings," 61–70; Stern, "The Team That Couldn't Be Beat," 25–41; and Voigt, "America's First Red Scare," 13–24.
9. *Daily Alta California,* June 16, 1870; Oakland *Daily News,* Dec. 2, 1872.
10. San Francisco *Chronicle,* Nov. 18, 1878.

11. *New York Clipper,* July 22, Aug. 12, and Aug. 19, 1876.

12. Hoie, "The Minor Leagues," 581.

13. Spalding, *Always on Sunday,* 14.

14. *Spalding's Official Baseball Guide* (1889), 58 (hereafter cited as *Spalding Guide*).

15. A resolution "for the suppression of obscene, indecent and vulgar language upon the ball field by players engaged in playing a game of ball during the championship season" was adopted by the National League on March 2, 1898.

16. See Franks, "Sweeney of San Francisco," 52–62.

17. *The Sporting Life* (1888), quoted in Franks, "The California League of 1886–1893," 54.

18. Quoted in Spalding, *Always on Sunday,* 80.

2

A New Show
on the West Coast

Mindful of the independent track that their circuit had taken for most of its history, and wary of the peace negotiations between the National and American leagues to end their bitter struggle, the men who contemplated a new direction for the California League after the 1902 season chose to continue to remain outside the reach of organized baseball. It was a practical decision as well, for the target cities of their expansionist designs—Portland and Seattle—were charter members of the Pacific Northwest League (PNL), a Class C operation within the fold of the National Association. The terms of that agreement protected franchise territories against encroachment by other parties to it. Ignoring the outcry of the PNL, though, the owners of the four clubs that had competed as the California League in 1901 and 1902 reconstituted themselves for the upcoming professional season and boldly challenged the far north league in its two principal locations. Resurrecting a name that two short-lived circuits had used previously, the barons of the West Coast game called their expanded organization the Pacific Coast League.

The new PCL immediately demonstrated a staying power far beyond that of its predecessors. Not only did the league establish competitive franchises in Portland and Seattle for the 1903 season, but it successfully fought off the attempt of the PNL (the "N" now stood for "National") to place teams of its own in Los Angeles and San Francisco. With such solid performers as Harry Lumley (Seattle, .387), Kid Mohler (Seattle, .314, 40 stolen bases), Kitty Brashear (Oakland and Seattle, .296), Truck Eagan (Sacramento, .326, 13 homers), Dan Shay (San Francisco, 83 stolen bases), Doc Newton (Los Angeles, 35-12), James Hughes (Seattle, 34-15), Warren Hall (Los Angeles, 32-18), Tom Thomas (Sacramento, 27-15), and Jimmy Whelan (San Francisco, 28-21) scattered among its member clubs, the PCL offered a better brand of ball than the PNL, which had diluted its rosters to field teams in the Coast League's two largest cities. Despite the runaway victory of the L.A. Angels—a 27½-game margin over runner-up Sacramento—the PCL emerged from its first season as the dominant league on the West Coast. The PNL retreated to the northwest, its California franchises having folded midway through the 1903 season and those in Tacoma and Helena disbanding at its end.[1]

Although the PCL was an instant success on the field, the rising costs of club operations influenced some major changes in the league's status and shape for its second season. Foremost among these was the decision to join the National Association, which awarded the league its highest designation, Class A. Engineered by PCL president Eugene Bert, the alliance with organized baseball recognized the quality of Coast League play, provided more national exposure for it, and sought to avoid the expensive bidding wars for players from the outlaw leagues. The owners searched for profits in other ways as well—for example, raising the price of a general admission ticket from twenty-five to thirty-five cents and reducing rosters from fifteen players to thirteen. Despite his team's second-place finish in the PCL's inaugural season, Sacramento manager Mique Fisher felt that even more drastic measures were necessary to strengthen the club's financial fortunes. He moved the franchise to the newly vacated park at South 11th and L streets in Tacoma. No longer sponsored by the brewers of Gilt Edge Beer, Fisher's boys were now the Tigers, and their play "proved they had sharp claws."[2] Powered by Eagan's twenty-five home runs and paced by the steady pitching of Robert Keefe (34-15) and Orval Overall (32-25), Tacoma gathered 130 wins against 94 losses and defeated Los Angeles five games to four in a play-off for the league title. The play-off, the first of many throughout the PCL's history, had been necessitated when the Tigers failed to win outright the second half of a split season. That arrangement had been introduced to maintain fan interest after L.A.'s romp the previous year.

Only two seasons into its operation, the PCL displayed many of the characteristics that would underscore its distinctiveness in the world of professional baseball. Most evident were the numbers, individual and team marks of glowing achievement and glaring ineptitude that were a statistician's delight: seasons extending to 220 or more games (Tacoma, Seattle, and Oakland played at least that number in 1904); team wins and losses exceeding 130 (Los Angeles won 133 in 1903; Portland lost 136 in 1904); batters accumulating over 900 plate appearances in a single season (George Van Haltren of Seattle registered 941 at bats in 1904); pitchers routinely starting 50 or more games a year (Oakland's Oscar Graham went 27-28 in 1903 in 59 starting assignments). Eagan's league-leading home run total in 1904 more than doubled the major league's

Runs,

Hits,

and

an Era

best of 10 homers by Harry Davis of the Philadelphia Athletics. Eagan, though, belted his 25 in 736 at bats, while Davis came to the plate a relatively modest 404 times. Shay's 83 stolen bases surpassed Honus Wagner's major league–leading total by 30, although the fleet-footed San Franciscan needed 215 games for his, the Flying Dutchman only 132. The long campaigns in the PCL also produced numbers that were less complimentary. Graham's moundswork in 1903 included 234 walks and 49 hit batsmen, single season records for wildness in both categories that have never been surpassed in the PCL. Contributing to Portland's last-place finish in 1904 were the team's 669 errors and .929 fielding percentage, records both unenvied and unmatched.

The game behind the numbers fully reflected the way the best professionals plied their trade around the turn of the century. The strategy of the day emphasized bat control, speed on the bases, and aggressiveness. Once the pitching distance had been moved from fifty feet to sixty feet, six inches in 1893, batting averages and run production had risen dramatically. Whereas team batting averages and runs per game were about .250 and five respectively, in the National League before the longer distance, they jumped to over .280 and seven for the rest of the 1890s. All minor leagues that adopted the NL's rules, including the California League, experienced a similar offensive explosion. Yet, it did not take long for the pitchers to recover. The advantages they had enjoyed in the shorter distance, such as the spitball, the "dead" ball, and the spacious dimensions of many ballparks behind them, continued into the twentieth century, while their greatest offset—deficiencies in team defense—became less a factor. Indeed, the poor playing surfaces, primitive fielding equipment (for his entire career Jerry Denny went about his chores without a glove), and virtually absent defensive strategy of the nineteenth-century game, which had placed additional burdens on even the most overpowering pitchers, were fading into memory.[3]

New defensive conditions, however, did not preclude continued reliance on a traditional practice: intimidation. The lone umpire usually assigned to games in the nineteenth century (and in the PCL until 1908) could only watch and control so much. Fielders employed all kinds of dirty tricks to impede runners' progress, tripping them as they ran by, grabbing their belts or loose uniform blouses to slow them down, or simply standing in their way on the base paths. Although few teams could match the violence and mean spirit that characterized the play of the Baltimore Orioles before the turn of the century, most infielders challenged runners with more than deft fielding. Crushing a hand reaching for a base with their sharpened spikes, throwing an elbow at a passing runner, or splitting a sliding player's lip with a viciously applied tag, they played a brand of ball that was not pretty. Yet it was the order of the day, "as gentlemanly," observed Ty Cobb, "as a kick in the crotch."[4]

Cobb's game not only inspired imitation but particularly appealed to those fans who encouraged mayhem on the fields. This was certainly no less the case in the West. Partners in a regional tradition that respected individual daring, appreciated neighborly interdependence, and tolerated occasional displays of wildness, western ballplayers and fans developed intimate and loyal relationships with each other that underscored the special spirit of the PCL. Such bonding between club and community was, of course, not unique to the Coast League. Minor league teams, largely because the game at this level maintains a nostalgic identity with grassroots America, have always managed to forge bonds with their local communities. But those between the PCL clubs and their cities were particularly strong. They were underscored in the curious distinction the league enjoyed of being both a minor and a major league at the same time—the former a matter of official classification, the latter the product of geography and western braggadocio.

The ballparks of the PCL particularly facilitated the communication between team and neighborhood. Shaped by the city blocks on which they were built, home to players who often lived in the same neighborhoods as the fans who went to see them play, and designed to accommo-

date spectators on the very edges of the field of play, the Coast League parks instilled images of community and democracy that were central tenets of the game's mystique. At many parks, fans could watch the local heroes perform from precarious perches just beyond the outfield fences in trees or on rooftops or billboards. Although the great PCL parks in Hollywood (Gilmore Field), Los Angeles (Wrigley Field), and San Francisco (Seals Stadium) were decades away from construction in 1904, the harmonious integration of the urban and the pastoral that they achieved already characterized several league playing grounds.

The best example of the neighborhood ballpark in the Coast League's early years was the Vaughn Street Ballpark in Portland. Situated on a rectangular site principally bounded by Vaughn, 24th Street, and 25th Avenue, it was built by two rival trolley companies that rightly assumed their cooperative venture would help both of their businesses. Accom-

The Vaughn Street Ballpark in Portland, Oregon, epitomized the neighborhood park on the West Coast. This 1951 view of the interior shows the expanded version of the grandstand. (#OrHi 26934. Oregon Historical Society.)

modating three thousand spectators for its opening in 1901 as the home of the old Northwest League's Portland entry, the park expanded to hold twice that number when the small wooden grandstand behind home plate was enlarged for track and field viewers at the 1905 Lewis and Clark Exposition. In the midst of four PCL pennants within five years, Portland owner Judge W. W. McCredie extended the covered grandstand along both baselines and added outfield bleachers in 1912, bringing the park's ultimate seating capacity to twelve thousand. With thick clouds of black smoke often wafting over the left field fence from the nearby Electric Steel Foundry, and long-time groundskeeper Rocky Benevento rushing throughout the stands with a water bucket to douse the ashes of cigarettes discarded on the old wood, the park and its friendly dimensions (331 feet down the left field line, 315 feet to right, 368 feet to a 20-foot-high fence in center) survived until 1955, when it was finally razed. Also known as Lucky Beavers Stadium, it was a throwback to another era that stood in sharp contrast to the multiuse, artificial turf facility that eventually replaced it.

The disaster that Benevento's bucket helped avoid in Portland visited San Francisco at 5:30 A.M. on the morning of April 18, 1906. Two weeks into the start of the PCL's fourth season, an earthquake registering 8.2 on

An aerial view of the Vaughn Street Ballpark, ca. 1955. (#OH 59089. Oregon Historical Society.)

the Richter scale rocked the San Andreas fault beneath the city for seventy long seconds. As buildings collapsed and water mains burst, devastating fires swept over four square miles in the center of the city, causing most of the nearly seven hundred deaths and $500 million in property damage. Among the casualties were the PCL's downtown league headquarters and the Seals' home field, Recreation Park, whose stands and offices burnt completely to the ground.

With three hundred thousand San Franciscans homeless and the city's infrastructure virtually destroyed, the status of the local ball club hardly seemed a matter of great concern to many. Yet, as would prove to be the case in times of war, depression, and urban violence that awaited the United States in the twentieth century, the need to provide people with a momentary escape from the crises of the daily headlines, to reassure them with the familiar rituals of normalcy, compelled the PCL to try to save the 1906 season. Coast League president Eugene Bert took the lead in this effort. Appealing to both the National Association and organized baseball for help, he received several thousand dollars from the National and American leagues for administrative operations and equipment. At a meeting with PCL executives two weeks after the earthquake, he persuaded them—particularly the financially strapped owners of the Los

San Francisco's devastation from the 1906 earthquake and fire is evident in this view of Van Ness and Sutter streets, a former hub of activity in the city. (The Oakland Museum Collection.)

J. Cal Ewing, owner of the Oakland Oaks, graciously opened Oakland's Idora Park to the San Francisco Seals for their home games after the 1906 earthquake. (The Oakland History Room, Oakland Public Library.)

Angeles Angels—to resume a full schedule of games. He had already arranged with Oakland Oaks owner J. Cal Ewing to move the Seals' home games to Oakland's Idora Park at 56th Street and Telegraph Avenue and to relocate the league's offices in downtown Oakland. Ewing, who was providing financial support to three other PCL clubs, contributed monetary resources as well to the Seals' relief effort. Indeed, by season's end, he had acquired a controlling interest in the club.

Sharply cutting payrolls and reducing its schedule from the 200-plus games of its initial seasons to around 180, the PCL limped through the year, although two franchises—Seattle and Fresno, the latter having only joined the league in 1906—folded at its conclusion. Behind league batting champ Mike Mitchell (.351) and player-manager Walter McCredie (.301), Portland won its first league title with a comfortable 20½-game margin over runner-up Seattle.

The second-place Indians owed their best showing in four PCL campaigns to the amazing performance of Harry "Rube" Vickers. A journeyman hurler acquired from Holyoke of the Connecticut League midway through the 1905 season after an unsuccessful shot at the majors with Cincinnati and Brooklyn in 1902–3 and a brief stint with Burlington in the outlaw Vermont League in 1904–5, Vickers suggested little in his checkered past of what he was about to accomplish for Seattle. Yet, in one of those shining seasons that occasionally elevate ordinary players to greatness, if only momentarily, the six-foot-two, 225-pound right-hander set the standard for ironman performance. Appearing in 64

Harry "Rube" Vickers, after a brief, unsuccessful try at the majors, joined the Seattle Indians midway through the 1905 season. A seemingly unremarkable pitcher, he would go on to set the all-time record for innings pitched in organized baseball in one spectacular season with the PCL before returning to the majors. (#Oreg 898. Oregon Historical Society.)

games, more than one-third of Seattle's season total, Vickers worked 526 innings, notched 408 strikeouts, and earned 39 victories against 20 defeats. His innings pitched remains the all-time record in organized baseball; his strikeouts and victories (the latter shared with Doc Newton, Los Angeles, 1904) stand as single season marks in the PCL. A year later Rube was back in the bigs pitching for Connie Mack's Philadelphia Athletics. On October 5, 1907, he touched brilliance again. In the first game of a doubleheader against Washington, Vickers pitched 12 innings of relief for the win; in the nightcap, he hurled 5 perfect innings for another victory. They were his only wins of the season. The workhorse of the A's staff in 1908 with an 18-19 record and a 2.34 ERA in 53 games, Vickers quickly faded after that, splitting 4 decisions in 18 games in 1909 before winding down his playing career with a few years in the Eastern and International leagues.

The league Vickers left behind on the West Coast, though, had demonstrated a remarkable strength of its own in recovering from the quake. Less than a year after the terrible trembler, ten thousand fans packed the new Recreation Park at 14th and Valencia streets in San Francisco for the 1907 opening day twin bill between the Seals and Portland.

Carlisle's Coup

One of the most extraordinary plays in baseball history occurred on July 19, 1911, in a game between the Los Angeles Angels and the visiting Vernon Tigers, when Walter Carlisle, Vernon's fleet-footed center fielder, made an unassisted triple play. Angels third baseman Roy Akin was at bat with teammates Charles Moore on second and George Metzger on first. Vernon pitcher Harry Stewart, just inserted, quickly got out of the jam when Akin hit a looping liner over the second baseman's head and Moore and Metzger took off "like a pair of scared jackrabbits." With the crowd on its feet, Carlisle raced in, dove for the ball, and rolled over three times while completing a circus catch. Realizing that Moore and Metzger were too far from their respective bags to return safely, he ran in and stepped on second, then trotted to first to complete the triple play. According to the San Francisco *Chronicle* of July 20, 1911, the fans "let out a roar that sounded like a mighty explosion. [They] stood on tiptoes, jumped from box to box, shrieked, threw up their hands and cheered for several minutes." Carlisle's feat was not in vain, as the Tigers triumphed 5-4.

They were there to celebrate not only the start of a new baseball season but their own progress in rebuilding their city. Rarely has the metaphor for hope that is baseball in the spring been clearer. Across the Bay, their fan base greatly enlarged with the resettlement of over sixty thousand San Franciscans in their city, the Oaks enjoyed a capacity house for their opener at Freeman's Park, their cozy home at 59th Street and San Pablo Avenue.

Neither the Seals nor the Oaks could translate civic pride into a PCL championship in the leaner, four-team league of 1907 and 1908. Los Angeles, winner of two of the first three PCL campaigns, added consecutive pennants in these years. Under the helm of player-manager Frank "Pop" Dillon, a cousin of New York Highlanders manager Clark Griffith, the Angels featured the league's strongest rotation in William "Dolly" Gray, who posted a 58-25 record over both championship seasons, and Judge Nagle and Frank Hosp, 24-10 and 20-15, respectively, in 1908. Walter Carlisle's league-leading 14 home runs and Gavvy Cravath's .303 bat and 10 home runs in 1907 provided enough offensive support for the staff. Except for Hosp, each of these players subsequently had opportunities with major league clubs. The most successful of the lot was Cravath, whose eleven-year career in the East began with the Boston Red Sox in 1908. Considering his impressive PCL record, Gray was probably the biggest disappointment among the former Angels in the majors. He spent three long years, from 1909 to 1911, compiling a 15-51 record with the lowly Washington Senators. No day was longer in Dolly's career—and none more reflective of his frustrations in the American League—than when he carried a one-hit shutout into the ninth inning of a game only to lose it on a two-out error and seven consecutive walks, all on 3-2 counts.

With Seattle's "Sea Lion" Hall, Emil Frisk, and Rube Walker, L.A.'s Hal Chase and Pop Dillon, Oakland's Oscar Graham, Tacoma's Orvall Overall, and the Seals' Roy Hitt having paved the way before them, Cravath,

Runs,

Hits,

and

an Era

William "Dolly" Gray, the gifted pitcher for the Los Angeles Angels, posted a 58-25 record that led his team through two consecutive PCL championships in 1907 and 1908. (National Baseball Library and Archive, Cooperstown, N.Y.)

The glove used by Vernon Tigers centerfielder Walter Carlisle during his unassisted triple play against the Los Angeles Angels on July 19, 1911. (Photograph by Doug McWilliams. Dick Dobbins Collection.)

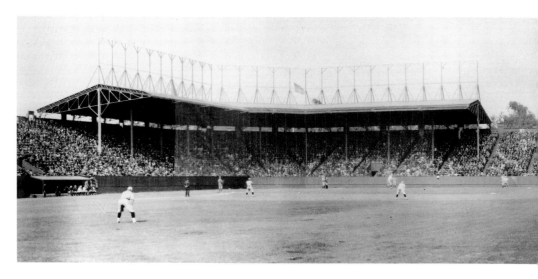

On May 16, 1914, opening day for the San Francisco Seals and their new ballpark, Ewing Field, 17,500 fans turned out to cheer their team on. (Swadly Photo, San Francisco. The Oakland Museum Collection.)

Gray, and the other Angels followed a steady stream of PCL alumni to the American and National leagues. For most of them, their stay was short, averaging just over three years on a major league roster. In this respect, the Pacific Coast League was no different from any other Class A minor league in the country. What began to set the PCL apart from its partners in the National Association, however, even at this early stage of its development, was the number of quality players it produced. "So many Coasters make good every season," observed Al Martin of *Baseball Magazine* in 1909, "that the Eastern magnates have come to regard the Pacific Coast League as the best developer of new players in the bushes." Ranking the PCL "next to the National and American Leagues" in the strength of its teams and the quality of their play, the writer found the Coast League second to none in the loyalty of its fans and the enthusiasm they displayed at its games. "The success of the league," he proclaimed, "was now fully established."[5]

Indeed, the evidence of that success took many forms. In 1909, the league returned to a six-team format with the addition of clubs from Sacramento and the Los Angeles suburb of Vernon. It would remain at that size for ten years, when expansion after the First World War raised the league's membership to eight, a number it maintained until 1962. The spinning turnstiles for PCL games not only supported expansion but also encouraged several owners to take steps to accommodate more fans in their clubs' ballparks. McCredie in Portland and William Curtin in Sacramento, for example, improved their existing grounds, adding and shading more seats under covered pavilions. Oakland's Ewing, however, felt that the time had come to build an entirely new park for his club, a

Interior of the Oaks' ballpark, Emeryville, California, ca. 1935. (Photograph by Moses Cohen. The Oakland Museum Collection.)

decision helped by its fine play in recent years and the deteriorating condition of Freeman's Park. Fielding teams that won over a hundred games in both 1910 and 1911, the Oaks finally captured their first PCL pennant in 1912 behind a solid pitching staff headed by Harry Ables (25-18, 303 strikeouts), Bill Malarkey (20-11), and Jack Killilay (15-4) and the offensive production of league MVP Gus Hetling (.297, 33 stolen bases), Bill Leard (80 stolen bases), and Bert Coy (19 homers). For opening day in 1913, Ewing rewarded them and their fans with what Chicago White Sox manager Nixey Callahan called "the finest minor league park west of Chicago."[6]

Built on a 465-foot-square lot at Park and San Pablo avenues in Emeryville, a small, sports-oriented community just north of Oakland, the new ballpark provided seating for nearly eleven thousand spectators, more than double what the Oaks' original home handled. Except for an arched canopy, which housed the announcer's and scorekeeper's booth and swept above the area directly behind home plate, the wooden stands were completely open to the sun. The dark green painted park and its rich grass field resembled a vast emerald set within a pewter border of streets and parking lots. Admitted to the bleachers for fifty cents, attended by vendors in natty blue uniforms with white piping, and

Graceful Exit

Though most fans would agree that the end of a baseball game can be a letdown after an afternoon or evening of excitement, Oakland fans enjoyed a special treat when leaving Oaks Park. The main exit was located in center field, so everyone got the chance to stroll over the "green carpet" their heroes had just vacated.

Brotherly Love

On April 7, 1918, "Doc" Crandall of the Los Angeles Angels, pitching the first game of a doubleheader against the Salt Lake City Bees, had a 4-0 lead and was one out away from a no-hitter. As fate would have it, Doc's brother Karl, the number three man in the Bees lineup, stepped up to the plate and hit a two-strike pitch for a single to ruin Doc's bid for fame. The Angels won the game on Doc's shutout, but Karl proved his hitting was no fluke as the Bees erupted for a 9-0 win in the nightcap, with Karl going four for four.

Eric Erickson, San Francisco Seals pitching sensation, was featured on a 1917 Zeenut series baseball card. (Dick Dobbins Collection.)

amused by the regulars in the right field stands who bet loudly on virtually every pitch and by the booming voice of "Mush the Ragman," who heaped abuse on Oakland's opponents, patrons of Oaks Park relished its charm and intimacy—if not the splintered souvenirs that the weathered seats increasingly gave up as the park aged. Outside the park, popular bars and restaurants, like Angelo's and Lindy's, catered to their working-class neighbors and the Oaks' family—fans and players whose similar social and economic status reinforced the community values that the game celebrated.

Perhaps the principal key to the Coast League's success under the new six-member format was its competitive balance. This translated into tight pennant races and the distribution of outstanding individual performances among all teams. From 1909 to 1918, five different clubs won pennants (half of them decided by margins of five games or fewer); and only one player (Harry Wolter, Los Angeles, .328 in 1914, .359 in 1915) took two batting titles and another (Bert Coy, Oakland, 19 in 1912, 18 in 1913) two home run crowns. No player led the league in stolen bases, strikeouts, or pitching victories for more than one season. The Angels' Doc Crandall came the closest in the latter category, notching twenty-six victories in 1917 to finish behind Eric Erickson's thirty-one wins for the Seals and sharing a league-high sixteen victories with Walt Leverenz of Salt Lake City in the war-shortened campaign of 1918.

For many of these seasons, a particularly memorable effort seemed to set its tone and influence its outcome. In 1909, the defining moment occurred on June 8 when Clarence "Cack" Henley of the Seals hooked up with Oakland's Jimmy Wiggs in "the greatest game ever seen west of the Rockies." For twenty-three innings and before an ever-growing "mob of howling fans," the two threw shutout ball, Henley giving up nine hits and a walk, Wiggs relinquishing eleven hits and six walks but striking out thirteen.[7] San Francisco finally won, 1-0, in the twenty-fourth inning on an unearned run. Organized baseball's longest shutout took just three and a half hours to complete. Henley rang up thirty more victories that season, against ten setbacks, as he and his workhorse partner on the Seals' mound, Frank Browning (32-16), paced the club to its first PCL championship. Henley's effort was no fluke. He posted a lifetime Coast League record of 212-171 over an eleven-year career, mostly with the Seals.

Outstanding pitching marked the deadball era as surely as Ty Cobb's flying spikes, and no team in any league enjoyed success for long without it. John McGraw's New York Giants ruled the National League in the early teens on the arms of Christy Mathewson, Rube Marquard, and Jeff Tesreau. The strongest clubs in the American League during the same period—Philadelphia and Boston—also boasted impressive staffs. Connie Mack's Athletics featured Jack Coombs, Ernie Plank, and Chief Bender; the Red Sox countered with Smoky Joe Wood, Dutch Leonard, Ernie

Shore, and, later, a big left-hander named Babe Ruth. The dominant team in the PCL from 1910 to 1914 was Portland, and it practiced well the winning formula of the day. Vean Gregg led the Beavers to their first of four league titles during this stretch with a 32-18 record in 1910. His wins included fourteen shutouts, a minor league record that still stands. Two of them came on the same day when he blanked Sacramento 4-0 in the first game of a doubleheader and then returned to shut the Sacs out 1-0 in the second.

Gregg signed with the Cleveland Indians in 1911 and went on to post three consecutive seasons of twenty or more wins, but Portland scarcely missed a beat without him. Bill Steen (30-15), Elmer Koestner (25-15), Tom Seaton (24-16), and Ed Henderson (21-12) pitched the Beavers to a second consecutive title, helped by Buddy Ryan's league-leading .333 batting average and twenty-three homers and the all-around play of shortstop Roger Peckinpaugh. With all of them except Koestner and Henderson in major league uniforms in 1912, Portland slipped to fourth place (Oakland won the pennant). The Beavers rebounded in 1913–14, though, again capturing back-to-back flags. Bill James (24-16, 215 strikeouts) and Irv Higginbotham (21-14) headed the staff one year; Higginbotham (31-20) and Hal Krause (22-18) the next. Gus Fisher handled the catching chores both years and added a solid bat to the lineup (.292 and .355). The most promising position player on the club, though, was a twenty-three-year-old infielder who had learned his lessons well from Peckinpaugh two seasons earlier. Nicknamed "Beauty" for the grace of his play, Dave Bancroft moved on to the Philadelphia Phils—and a Hall of Fame career—the following year.

The Seals spoiled Portland's hopes for an unprecedented third straight title in 1915. Relying on the play of local products Spider Baum (30-15, 2.45 ERA), Harry Heilmann (.364), and Ping Bodie (.325, 19 homers), San Francisco finished atop the standings with a five-game margin over a PCL newcomer, the Salt Lake City Bees. The convergence of these stars on the Seals' roster reflected the full range of paths that a professional ballplaying career could take as the league grew in prestige. At one end

Runs,

Hits,

and

an Era

of the spectrum was Baum, who typified the many Coast Leaguers who declined major league offers, preferring instead to spend their entire careers on western diamonds. The slim right-hander played nineteen years in the minors, fifteen in the PCL, where he won 262 games. His lifetime professional record of 325-280 included nine seasons with twenty or more wins. Only Frank Shellenback had more pitching victories (295) in the PCL. At the other end was Heilmann. Purchased by the Detroit Tigers in 1914 from Portland of the Northwest League after only one season of ball, Harry was with the Seals in 1915 for further seasoning. His strong bat overshadowed a weak glove and he returned to Detroit a year later, a short 98-game career in the PCL forever behind him. Leading the American League in hitting on three occasions, Heilmann finished a seventeen-year major league career with a .342 batting average and a plaque in Cooperstown.

Bodie split the difference—nine years in the PCL, nine in the American League. Born Francesco Stephano Pezzolo, Bodie took his surname from the California town where his father once worked as a miner; "Ping" derived from the sound of his bat on the ball. In 1910 the sound was particularly noticeable as Bodie led all of organized baseball with thirty home runs for the Seals. That performance earned him a contract with the Chicago White Sox, but a declining batting average after two promising years sent him back to the Seals in time for their PCL championship in 1915. Two consecutive seasons hitting above .300 earned Bodie another shot at the majors, first with the Athletics and then four years as a Yankee. In New York, Bodie roomed for a while with Ruth—or, as he once corrected a reporter who inquired about that experience, "I don't actually room with Ruth; I room with his suitcase." A favorite with the press wherever he played, the good-natured Californian served as a model for Ring Lardner's ballplayer-narrator in the "You Know Me Al" stories. Another columnist found that one of Bodie's few weaknesses as a player, his slowness afoot, still made good copy. Watching Ping get thrown out by several yards on an attempted steal, Arthur Baer wrote: "He had larceny in his heart, but his feet were honest." Ping completed his playing career with the San Francisco Missions in 1928, when, at age forty-one, he stroked the ball for a .348 average.

Streaking Acorn

In 1915 Jack Ness, captain and slugging first baseman for the Oakland Oaks, hit safely in what was then a PCL and professional baseball record forty-nine consecutive games. Jack's hitting eclipsed the PCL mark of twenty-eight held by Chester Chadbourne and the major league record of forty-four set by Willie Keeler in 1897. Jack's streak began on Memorial Day 1915 against the Vernon Tigers and ended on July 22 against the same Vernon squad, when pitcher Art Fromme sent him to the dugout with no hits in four attempts. In game 8 of the streak, Ness had been inserted as a pinch hitter and had only one at bat to keep his streak alive, and he responded with a hit. During the forty-nine-game streak, he collected seventy-nine hits and boasted a .457 average. His PCL mark held until 1933, when a young Joe DiMaggio hit in sixty-one consecutive games.

Bay Area native Harry Heilmann helped lead the San Francisco Seals to the pennant in 1915 with a .364 batting average. (#Oreg 352. Oregon Historical Society.)

Born Francesco Stephano Pezzolo, San Francisco Seals power hitter "Ping" Bodie took his last name from the California town of Bodie and his first from the sound of the ball as it hit the bat. Photograph ca. 1915. (#Oreg 1231. Oregon Historical Society.)

While prosperity and a rising competitive reputation accompanied the Pacific Coast League through the mid-1910s, the "Eastern Leagues," as the PCL owners and supporters derisively called the major leagues, were experiencing a period of sustained crisis. It began in 1914 with the launching of the Federal League, an eight-team circuit that claimed "major" league status and dangled attractive salary offers before the players of the American and National leagues to prove it.[8] With few exceptions, the owners of the older leagues prevented the defections of "name" players to the Federal clubs, but it cost them dearly. Enjoying a rare advantage at the bargaining table with a management that feared losing them, major league players won salary increases and concessions on such issues as severance pay, working conditions, and reentry negotiating rights.

Despite a close pennant race and fair attendance figures in most of its cities, the Federal League incurred huge financial losses and a sizable long-range debt in the construction of new ballparks for several of its franchises. The infusion of new capital from oil millionaires Harry Sinclair and P. J. White and the expectation of a favorable decision in an antitrust suit against organized baseball carried the Federal League into a second season in 1915. The deep pockets and unified resistance of the major league owners, however, were too much for the Feds to overcome. The new league formally folded in December 1915, and the victors moved quickly to recover the costs of protecting their monopoly. Containing the market for player talent and eliminating their eastern competition for the baseball gate, the major league owners systematically cut payrolls and ignored other player interests.

Since the Federal League had concentrated its roster raiding on the major leagues and such minor circuits as the International League, the American Association, and the Southern League, the PCL experienced no unusual patterns in player movement in 1914–15. Such was not the case in a crisis of far greater proportions: the American entrance into the war that had been raging in Europe since August 1914. President Woodrow Wilson's address to Congress calling for a declaration of war against Germany came on April 2, 1917, a few weeks into the Coast League's new season. Except for a handful of volunteers, rosters were not significantly affected by that summer's draft calls. PCL players joined the nearly ten million American males between the ages of twenty-one and thirty-five who registered in the military census of early June, but bureaucratic inefficiency and operational problems with the entire war mobilization effort virtually ensured that no players would be called to active duty before the end of the season. As a result, the PCL, like the major leagues

A

New

Show

on the

West

Coast

and the more established minor circuits, survived the first year of the country's formal participation in World War I. Led by Eric Erickson's pitching Triple Crown (31-15, 1.93 ERA, 307 strikeouts), San Francisco won its second pennant in three seasons, narrowly preventing Los Angeles from winning consecutive titles under player-manager Frank Chance, the former "Peerless Leader" of the Chicago Cubs.

Soon, ominous signs foretold an end to the prosperity that professional baseball had been enjoying for many years. Attendance had fallen off at ballparks across the nation as popular attention focused on the struggle "over there" and as new forms of entertainment—motion pictures, automobile driving, and other spectator sports, especially football—competed for the public's leisure dollars. Whereas forty-two minor leagues had been operating in 1914, only twenty started the 1917 season and only twelve completed it. The PCL cut its rosters from twenty to sixteen players in a cost-savings step, but more drastic measures would be necessary if the league hoped to survive another season in wartime.

No Hits, No Wins

Frank Arellanes of the Solons pitched a no-hitter on October 10, 1910, but lost to the Vernon Tigers 2-0. Nearly four years later, on September 10, 1914, Portland Beaver hurler John Lush shared Arellanes's bad fortune and lost a no-hitter to the Venice Tigers by a score of 1-0.

With the two major leagues and only eight other minor leagues, the PCL attempted to give it a go in 1918. Curtailing its preseason and replacing Portland with a team in Sacramento to reduce travel expenses, the league started play but quickly encountered a hurdle too great to overcome. On May 23, United States Provost Marshall Enoch Crowder ordered all draft-eligible men to find work deemed essential for the war effort or face induction. Although the major leagues received a temporary dispensation from the notice to complete their own shortened season by Labor Day, the PCL did not. Draft boards in California and Utah, concerned about the public's reaction to the sight of able-bodied men playing a game for a living while the country went to war to make the world safe for democracy, upheld the "work or fight" directive for ballplayers. Meeting in Los Angeles on Saturday, July 13, the directors of the Pacific Coast League agreed to end the season that weekend. Although Vernon held a narrow lead over Los Angeles at the time (58-44, compared to the Angels' 57-47), league officials decided that a best-of-nine play-off series between the two teams would determine the champion. With spitballer Doc Crandall maintaining the regular season form that produced a league-leading sixteen victories, the Angels won the play-off five games to two for their sixth PCL pennant.

Considering that only one minor league circuit, the International League, avoided the termination of the 1918 season before its scheduled completion, the PCL performed well in the dire circumstances of wartime. Its truncated season ended with some semblance of order and

Runs,

Hits,

and

an Era

The ceremonial raising of the U.S. flag marks the beginning of the 1918 baseball season at San Francisco's Recreation Park. (California State Library.)

heightened regard for its basic strengths, foremost of which were effective league management, established player talent, and a broad fan base. All were critical as the league—and organized baseball in general—nervously approached the 1919 season, the first after the great war. Little did the league and the larger baseball world in which it operated anticipate the prosperity—and perils—that lay ahead in the next decades.

Notes

1. Historical accounts of the Pacific Coast League include O'Neal, *The Pacific Coast League;* Blake, *The Minor Leagues,* 123–42; and Obojski, *Bush League,* 137–83.
2. Martin, "The Pacific Coast League," 39.
3. On baseball strategy in the 1890s, see Felber, "The Changing Game," 270–74; James, *Historical Baseball Abstract,* 38–40; and Alexander, *John McGraw,* 25–26.
4. Cobb, *My Life in Baseball,* 41.
5. Martin, "The Pacific Coast League," 42.
6. Dedication Program, Oakland Baseball Club, 1913, author's files.
7. San Francisco *Chronicle,* June 9, 1909.
8. For a brief history of the Federal League, see Okkonen, *The Federal League of 1914–1915,* 1.

Runs,

Hits,

and

an Era

3

Roaring in the Twenties

The armistice of November 1918 brought an end to the fighting overseas, but there were few signs of the peaceful millennium that Woodrow Wilson had promised would begin at Versailles. While the president enjoyed accolades in Europe, pent-up frustrations with wartime shortages and inconveniences and impatience with the reconversion process to a peacetime economy and social order revived old tensions and revealed new antagonisms at home. Nearly five million Americans went to war, but many found no jobs waiting for them when they returned. Often they found their old jobs filled by southern blacks who had migrated northward to find work in urban factories, or by immigrants who were unaffected by the military draft. The curtailment of government contracts produced massive layoffs in war production industries and added to the workers' troubles. Those who had jobs faced reductions in their paychecks and rising prices at the market. The bitterness of jobless veterans turned to violence throughout the country. Ugly race riots in Arkansas, Texas, and several northern cities dramatized the anger of white workers toward their new competitors in the labor market. Shocking the nation as much as these incidents did was a wave of strikes that rolled across the land in 1919. Over twenty-six hundred of them, including a general strike in Seattle that shut down the city for nearly a week, involved more than four million workers.

Much of the blame for these developments focused on political dissidents in the United States who rallied to the flag of Bolshevism. Seattle's mayor, for example, raged that his city was in the grip of a "red revolution."[1] Attorney General A. Mitchell Palmer sounded the alarm of a national "Red Scare" and urged nativist and patriotic groups to carry forward their wartime animosity toward nonconformists and dissenters in a new campaign against radicals and aliens. Organizations such as the Loyal American League, the Association for Constitutional Government, and the Sons of the American Revolution welcomed Palmer's words and

Georges Clemenceau of France (left), President Woodrow Wilson (center), and Prime Minister Lloyd George leave the Palace of Versailles after signing the historic peace treaty that brought an end to World War I. (The Oakland Museum Collection.)

attracted large memberships united in the desire to promote "American" values and institutions. The symbols of the American spirit—historical landmarks, the Constitution, the flag—became special objects of veneration. Some groups, like the Ku Klux Klan, pursued the concept of a homogenous Americanism to violent extremes, but most focused on more comfortable and less threatening ways to demonstrate their national pride and identity. No place, suggested an editorial in *The Sporting News*, offered Americans greater prospect "to keep a lot of us out of trouble . . . [during these] ticklish times than the ball park."[2]

Although the doughboys had returned from Europe and the ballplayers among them were back in the fold of their prewar clubs, most major and minor league baseball owners initially anticipated another lean year in 1919. The American and National league operators agreed to keep their preseason training schedules within the self-imposed limits of the previous year, restrict the new campaign to 140 games, limit club payrolls, and reduce rosters from twenty-five to twenty-one players. The Pacific Coast League clubs planned conservatively in some matters, restor-

PCL vs. the American Association

The Vernon Tigers, 1919 champions of the PCL, and the St. Paul Saints, 1919 champions of the American Association, two evenly matched teams, squared off in a best-of-nine contest labeled the "Little World Series." All games were played in Los Angeles at Washington Park. After eight games the series was tied at four apiece, and game 9 was deadlocked in the eighth inning at 1-1. "Wheezer" Dell of Vernon knocked in the deciding run in the ninth and also went the distance in pitching the Tigers to a 2-1 series victory in the finale.

The series was typical of the deadball era when runs were at a premium and fisticuffs were part of the game. Umpires were not immune from the fighting and actually became active participants in the brawls in the 1919 series. In game 3 of the series, won by Vernon (2-1), a near riot took place at the end of the sixth inning when an umpire named Murray of the American Association called a Vernon player out on a close play at first. Manager Bill Essick ran out to protest and was quickly followed by his players. One of the Tigers struck the umpire, who returned the blow, and the ensuing melee had to be broken up by police officers. Game 5, which Vernon also won 2-1, was marred by a fight. According to the San Francisco *Chronicle* of October 13, 1919, there were "several tilts between the Saints and Umpire Toman who was behind the plate. Toman's chest guard was torn from him and he was struck several times in an argument in the fifth inning."

The Little World Series was played again in 1924 when the same St. Paul Saints came west to play the PCL champion Seattle Indians, led by hard-hitting Brick Eldred. St. Paul won the opening game of the series, but the balance of the games were canceled due to inclement weather. The final series between the PCL and AA took place the next season when Louisville lost to the PCL champion San Francisco Seals five games to four.

ing, for example, average schedules to only 180 games, about 25 short of the prewar seasons. They gambled boldly in other areas, though, most notably deciding to readmit clubs from Portland and Seattle, thus increasing the circuit to eight teams for the new campaign. Recalling the rapid recovery of the league after the 1906 earthquake, PCL president Allan Baum and league officials sensed that fan interest would support a larger structure.

The big crowds that turned out for the PCL games in the early going proved that league officials were right. A cross-Bay doubleheader on April 20, for example, involving a morning game in Oakland and an afternoon game in San Francisco between the Oaks and the Seals, drew almost twenty-four thousand fans. On the same day, a similar two-game set between Los Angeles and Vernon attracted another twenty-five thousand. Moreover, the same was occurring across the nation. Spectators were filling ballparks in numbers that had not been seen in years,

Roaring in the Twenties

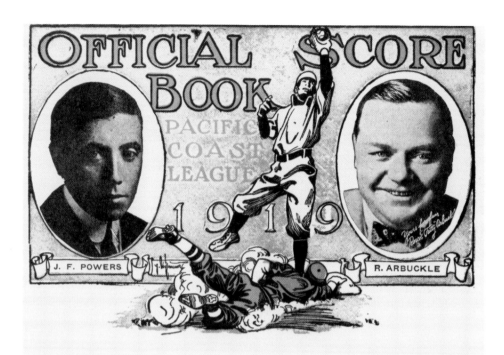

The official 1919 score book for the Hollywood Stars, featuring the film star (and later owner of the Stars) Fatty Arbuckle (right). (Bob Reiss.)

prompting Irving Sanborn of *The Spalding Guide* to write that "even the most pronounced optimist could not fail to be surprised by the quick recovery in popular estimation made by professional Base Ball in 1919."[3]

Notwithstanding the revolving turnstiles and the attempts of baseball magnates and publicists to celebrate the game's alleged reflection of the best American virtues, all was not well on the nation's diamonds. Although gambling, bribery, and game-fixing scandals had plagued professional ball from its beginnings, prompting one nineteenth-century Buffalo writer to observe that "a horse race is a pretty safe thing to speculate on, in comparison with an average ball match," the baseball world was still unprepared for the shocking revelations about the 1919 World Series.[4] Claiming that he had "lived a thousand years in the last twelve months" harboring his guilt and fending off accusations about his play in the loss to the underdog Cincinnati Reds, Chicago White Sox pitcher Eddie Cicotte unfolded a lurid tale of corruption and deceit to a grand jury in Cook County, Illinois, on September 28, 1920, about how he and seven other teammates had conspired to throw the series. Relying primarily on the testimony of Cicotte and "Shoeless Joe" Jackson, the grand jury returned indictments for fraud against eight White Sox players and five others for their roles in arranging the fix. By the time the so-called Black Sox finally came to trial in June 1921, however, the prosecution's case had been essentially destroyed with the mysterious disappearance of the players' original confessions. Repudiating what they had said earlier, the players gave the jury little hard evidence on which to convict them of the charge of "conspiracy to commit an illegal act."[5] On August 2, the jury returned a verdict of not guilty.

The decision of the Chicago court was not the judgment of organized baseball. The very next day, Judge Kennesaw Mountain Landis, in office barely nine months as the game's first commissioner, issued his opinion in the matter. "Regardless of the verdict of juries," Landis declared, "no player who throws a ball game, no player that undertakes or promises to throw a ball game, no player that sits in a conference with a bunch of crooked players and gamblers where the ways and means of throwing a game are discussed and does not promptly tell his club about it, will ever play professional baseball."[6] Hired to convince the country that the integrity of the national pastime had been restored beyond any doubt, Landis permanently banned the Chicago eight from the game.

The harshness of the commissioner's decision surprised many as much as did the initial revelations about the fixed series. The PCL knew better on both counts. Not only had the league already had its share of crooked behavior, but it had addressed it in a manner that provided an example for Landis.

The open gambling that took place in the right-field stands of Oaks Park acknowledged common practice throughout the league. The issue was not that betting on Coast League games took place but whom it involved and whether it affected play on the field. Acting on evidence that the 1919 season had been particularly tainted with bribes and thrown games, the league's new president, William H. McCarthy, launched an investigation that produced criminal charges against several players. Most prominent among them were Salt Lake City outfielders Bill Rumler, the season's batting champion with a .362 average, and Harl Maggert, who led the league with 127 runs scored. Others included Vernon first baseman Babe Borton (.303), Seals pitcher Casey Smith (17-19), and the veteran Portland hurler Tom Seaton (25-16). The most serious charges against the players alleged that they had either offered or accepted bribes to drop games that helped Vernon win the pennant. Although a Los Angeles grand jury failed to issue indictments against the players in October 1920, McCarthy felt that decisive action was necessary to clear away any lingering clouds of scandal. Providing a precedent for Landis, he summarily expelled from the league all players who had been suspected of wrongdoing in the affair.

To no one's surprise, implicated in both the PCL scandal and the 1919 World Series fix was California's Hal Chase, perhaps the most unsavory professional ballplayer after the turn of the century. Until his ultimate suspension from the game while playing for the New York Giants in 1919, "Prince Hal" displayed a penchant for crookedness as impressive as his glove work around first base. Recalling the fights that Chase frequently instigated while he played for Bay Area teams between major league campaigns and his perverse pride in stealing cigars and other small items, Harry Hooper, who had left Sacramento in 1909 for the Boston Red Sox and a Hall of Fame career, concluded that Hal "just wasn't all there."[7] Nevertheless, Chase cavorted through fifteen major league seasons betting on games in which he played, conspiring with teammates to throw games, bribing opponents, and practicing petty thievery while the baseball establishment largely looked the other way. Escaping trial in Chicago when California law did not permit his extradition to Illinois, Chase was caught in McCarthy's net and banned for life from PCL ballparks.

The manner in which the major leagues and the PCL addressed the corruptness on their playing fields restored public confidence in the game and, as much as the home runs that boomed from the bats of Babe Ruth and his protégés, ushered in one of baseball's golden eras. Throughout the 1920s, all levels of organized baseball enjoyed the benefits of a

Runs,

Hits,

and

an Era

46

PCL president William H. McCarthy resolved a 1919 gambling scandal by expelling all players suspected of wrongdoing. His decisive action helped to restore public confidence in the game and allowed the league to take full advantage of the 1920s baseball boom. (FN-29910. California Historical Society, San Francisco.)

Portland pitcher Tom Seaton was one of several players ousted from the league by the PCL president. He was suspected of accepting a bribe to help the Vernon Tigers win the 1919 championship. (#Oreg 796. Oregon Historical Society.)

"Prince Hal" Chase, a former PCL first baseman, was possibly the shadiest professional ballplayer after the turn of the century, as crooked off the field as he was
talented on it. His penchant for gambling, fighting, and thievery led to his suspension in 1919 from both major and minor league play. (National Baseball Library
and Archive, Cooperstown, N.Y.)

strong national economy, an expanding urban population, declining
work hours, and greater consumer spending on recreation, which
approached $5 billion annually by the end of the decade. In 1919,
fourteen minor leagues launched schedules; by mid-decade, twenty-four
such circuits, as well as the Negro National League, were flourishing.
None, however, was more successful or important—or more colorful—
than the Pacific Coast League.

The PCL offered something for everyone: tight pennant races, heroic
performances, zany characters, great ballparks, stable franchises, intense
rivalries, dazzling pitching, and spectacular hitting. Make that *awesome*
hitting. With the ban of the spitball and other trick pitches, more unifor-
mity and the use of higher quality yarns in the manufacture of baseballs,

Runs,

Hits,

and

an Era

greater frequency in introducing new balls during games, improved backdrops for hitters in many parks, and the growing popularity of Ruth's swing-from-the-heels batting style, the 1920s witnessed a permissiveness at the plate throughout professional baseball even greater than that following the lengthening of the pitching distance in 1893. Major league batting averages, for example, rose overall from .248 in 1916 to .292 in 1925. Not surprisingly, so did earned run averages, increasing from 2.71 to 4.33 over the same ten years. This was the decade of Ruth's 60 home runs (1927) and .847 slugging percentage (1920), Rogers Hornsby's .424 batting average (1924), Lou Gehrig's 175 RBIs (1927), and Lefty O'Doul's 254 hits (1929). No batting title in either major league was won with less than a .353 average, and six times the batting champ hit over .400. Impressive figures to be sure, though the mighty bats of the PCL players produced heftier ones.

"Big Earl" Sheely, a slow-moving but sure-handed first baseman who began his Coast League career with Salt Lake City, bracketed an eight-year stay in the majors with PCL seasons that claimed batting and home run crowns in 1920 (.371 and 33) and another hitting title plus the league's highest RBI output in 1930 (.403 and 180). Only once during the decade (Hack Miller, Oakland, 1921, .347) would Sheely's lowest batting title average have led the league, yet his highest was surpassed twice (Smead Jolley, San Francisco, 1928, .404; Ike Boone, Missions, 1929, .407). After 1922, the PCL home run champions averaged almost 47 a season through the rest of the decade, including Tony Lazzeri's 60 in 1925, a number certainly assisted by a 200-game schedule and the thin desert air of Salt Lake. Like his 222 RBIs and 202 runs scored in the same season, these are marks unsurpassed in the league's record books. Aside from the 467 round-trippers that Ruth hit from 1920 to 1929, the mere mortals who claimed home run titles in the National League only averaged 31 a season.

No day more clearly signaled the PCL's participation in the era of the lively ball than May 11, 1923, when Vernon and Salt Lake City, two teams headed for losing records that season, met at the Bees' Bonneville Park. Tallying four runs in their first turn at bat, the visiting Californians served notice that they had come to play. Three innings later they had built a 20-4 lead. Then they got serious. Scoring a modest four more runs in the sixth, Vernon nearly batted around its order twice in the seventh, adding eleven runs to its game-ending total of thirty-five.

Leading the Tigers' hit parade was right fielder Pete Schneider, who had returned to the West Coast after pitching for seven years in the majors with the Cincinnati Reds and the New York Highlanders. Vernon converted Schneider to an outfielder to get his decent bat (.289 with the Reds in 1918) into the lineup on a regular basis. No bat in the history of the league treated a ball more unkindly than his did this day. Coming to bat eight times, Schneider belted five home runs, including two grand

In 1925, Tony Lazzeri, Salt Lake City's super slugging shortstop, broke all-time PCL records for home runs, RBIs, and runs scored. He knocked out sixty homers in one season, two years before Babe Ruth would do the same in the major leagues. (National Baseball Library and Archive, Cooperstown, N.Y.)

Runs,
Hits,
and
an Era

slams, and a double. His hits drove in fourteen runs, amassed twenty-two total bases, and carried him across the plate six times. His record-setting performance in all these categories would have been even more phenomenal had not his bid for a sixth home run in his last at bat fallen short of clearing the fence by inches. Schneider's offensive display, joined with twenty-seven hits by his teammates and the Bees' own eleven runs, rang up combined game totals of forty-six runs and forty-eight hits. Ironically, although Schneider finished the season with a .360 batting average, he only managed fourteen homers in the other 200 games he played, placing his total far behind the league-leading forty-three clouted by another former pitcher, Salt Lake's Paul Strand.

After winning six games for Boston's "Miracle Braves" in 1914, Strand suffered arm trouble, converted to the outfield, and spent time in several minor circuits until the Bees acquired him in 1921. A year later, he led the PCL in batting (.384), home runs (28), and RBIs (138). In 1923 he did it again, increasing his batting average ten points, his RBIs by forty-nine, and his homers by fifteen. The 325 hits he accumulated to capture his second consecutive Triple Crown established an all-time record in organized baseball.

Just as the performances of Schneider and Strand underscored the offensive capabilities of their clubs, the forty-six runs their pitching gave up that long day in the desert revealed the principal reason why neither the Tigers nor the Bees were pennant winners after 1920. Although Salt Lake City had failed to capture any PCL flags since joining the league in 1916, while Vernon had won three consecutive regular season championships from 1918 to 1920, the Tigers had actually fallen on harder times in the new decade. In 1923 and 1925, Vernon finished last in the standings, losing 120 or more games each season. After sub-.500 seasons in four of the last five years, Salt Lake City had rallied to a second-place finish in 1925

Peter Schneider of the Vernon Tigers was featured on this 1923 Zeenut series baseball card. In one game against the Salt Lake City Bees, on May 11, 1923, the former pitcher turned right fielder came to bat eight times for a double and five home runs, including two grand slams. (Dick Dobbins Collection.)

on the strength of Lazzeri's run production and the solid bat work of another former pitcher, Lefty O'Doul. Returning to the Coast League in 1924 with a sore arm after an unsuccessful year with the Red Sox, O'Doul failed to regain the pitching form that had won twenty-five games for the Seals in 1921. Focusing his attention on his hitting, Lefty found the stroke that eventually would carry him back to the majors as an outfielder for seven more seasons, including two as NL batting champion. He warmed up for those performances with a .375 batting average and 191 RBIs in 1925 for the Bees.

Absence from pennant contention aggravated the long-standing problem of a limited fan base in both Salt Lake City and Vernon and effected the only franchise shifts the Pacific Coast League would make between 1919 and 1936. His old gold miner's instincts directing him to new fields to prospect, Bill Lane moved his Utah boys to Hollywood, changed their name to the Stars, and arranged for them to share the Angels' newly constructed ballpark, Wrigley Field. Although located in south central L.A., about nine miles from Hollywood and Vine, Wrigley served as the Stars' home for ten seasons. Meanwhile, Vernon owner Edward Maier was concluding a similar deal for his club. Finding backers in San Francisco who felt that their city could support two PCL teams, he transferred the franchise north, where it resurrected the Missions name. As the original Missions had done in 1914, the new club shared Recreation Park with the Seals, a cotenancy that would carry over to Seals Stadium after its opening in 1931.

Once the dust had settled and the suitcases were unpacked, the PCL had an alignment that fostered rivalries in every direction. The three-way struggle among the Seals, Oaks, and Missions for Bay Area bragging rights fully matched the heat generated among the Giants, Dodgers, and Yankees for similar claims in the New York metropolitan area. Few victories pleased Sacramento more than those over the Bay Area clubs—prickly reminders that the northern California baseball world extended beyond view of the Golden Gate. Seattle and Portland, of course, competed against each other for the supremacy of the Northwest yet delighted in each other's triumphs over the Californians. Similarly, the Angels and the Stars feuded locally and widely, vying for fans and flags in Wrigley, yet together fending off the invaders from the North.

What made these many-layered rivalries so intense was the distribution of player talent and the taste of competitive success—and failure—for all teams in the league. From 1920 to 1930, seven different clubs won Coast League championships; only two, Los Angeles (1921, 1926) and San Francisco (1922, 1923, 1925, 1928), captured more than one. At the other end of the standings, six teams, including the Angels and the Seals, finished last at least once during this period. Portland, which failed to win a championship in these years, was the sole team to anchor the league more than twice (1920, 1921, 1930).

The Seals' four championships in the 1920s underscored the league's most successful franchise. Only once during the decade—1926—did the club fail to finish in the first division or win at least one hundred games. Averaging 112 wins a season, San Francisco amassed 102 more victories (1,120) than Los Angeles, its most consistent challenger for PCL honors. Reasonably stable rosters, steady pitching, and a thunderous offense keyed the Seals' winning ways.

Babe Ellison and Smead Jolley, although their careers in San Francisco overlapped for just one championship in 1925, typified the club's ability to field strong teams year after year. Ellison joined the Seals in 1921 after the Detroit Tigers had tried him in every outfield and infield position over the course of five mostly part-time seasons. Settling in at first base, Babe began to light up the league with his hitting. Stroking .311 in his first year on the coast, he added a .306 batting average and 141 RBIs to the Seals' pennant-winning lineup of 1922. The club signaled its appreciation of his numbers and leadership in naming him manager for the next campaign. Ellison delivered both in and out of the dugout. Over the next three seasons, he averaged .356 at the plate (.381 in 1924), drove in 487 runs, including a league best 188 in 1924, and belted 78 homers. Three of his 33 round-trippers in 1924 came in consecutive games against the still-belea-

> ### The Longest Home Run
>
> Though fireworks could be seen lighting up the Bay Area sky on the Fourth of July in 1929, none seemed to travel as high or as far as that day's home run by Oakland's Roy Carlyle. In the fourth inning of the second game of the holiday doubleheader against the San Francisco Missions, Carlyle came up to bat against Ernie Nevers, a Stanford alumnus and eventual pro football Hall of Famer, and hit a towering drive that cleared the fence in centerfield, just to the right of the clubhouse.
>
> Though all present would attest that Carlyle's blast was of no ordinary nature, it was not officially measured until three days later when a teammate, who said he saw the ball land, gathered a group of people to measure the Herculean shot. The ball had flown over two rooftops and landed in the rain gutter of a third house, an amazing 618 feet from home plate—arguably the longest *measured* home run in professional baseball history. A plaque can still be seen at the site of the demolished Oaks Park commemorating the shot. Not well known for tape-measure homers (ironically, the Oaks' long-ball specialist, Buzz Arlett, was on deck at the time of Carlyle's smash), Roy Carlyle finished his career with 119 home runs.

guered pitching of Salt Lake City. As a field general, Ellison guided his team to two league titles in 1923 and 1925 and a narrow second-place finish behind Seattle in 1924.

Jolley joined the Seals for the final weeks of the 1925 championship season after leading Corsicana of the Texas Association with 174 hits and 24 home runs. Although there was little room for him initially in a San Francisco outfield that featured Paul Waner (.401), the league's best hitter, in left, Gene Valla (.333) in center, and Frank "Turkeyfoot" Brower (.362, 36 homers, 163 RBIs) in right, Smead posted numbers that no one could ignore. In only thirty-eight games for the Seals, the six-foot-three

Oakland Oaks power-hitting outfielder Roy Carlyle hit one of the longest home runs in professional baseball history on July 4, 1929. Three days later, a teammate arranged to measure the distance the ball had traveled—over two rooftops and into the rain gutter of a house 618 feet away from home plate. (The Oakland Tribune Collection.)

San Francisco outfielder Smead Jolley averaged over thirty-four home runs and 160 RBIs in four seasons with the Seals before moving on to the major leagues. (National Baseball Library and Archive, Cooperstown, N.Y.)

powerhouse collected 59 hits, including 12 home runs, that produced a gaudy .447 batting average. Before heading to the White Sox after the 1929 season, Smead pasted PCL pitching at a .388 clip. During his four full seasons with the Seals, he also averaged over 34 home runs and 160 RBIs per campaign. Leading the league in hitting (.397) and RBIs (163) in 1927, he added to those figures in 1928 (.404 and 188), blasted a league-high 45 home runs, and came away with a Triple Crown. Even in the majors, Jolley managed a solid .305 lifetime batting average.

But the big man was flawed: his Triple A hitting was plagued with Class D fielding. Although the eastern press probably exaggerated Smead's shortcomings, forty-four errors in only 413 outfield games in the majors suggested some basis for the criticism. One story, albeit undocumented, particularly ridiculed his defensive skills. Playing right field one afternoon, Smead allegedly let a hard-hit ball pass through his legs for an error. Turning to retrieve the ball, he encountered it coming back at him off the wall, whereupon it went through his legs again for a second error. Finally catching up with it, he threw wildly over the head of his in-

Future Hall of Famer Earl Averill was part of San Francisco's triple-threat outfield, which included Smead Jolley and Roy Johnson. Their playing prowess brought the Seals from a last-place finish in 1926 to the championship in 1928. (San Francisco History Room, San Francisco Public Library.)

tended target for his third error—all on a single play. Still, teams in nine different minor leagues over the course of a twenty-year professional career were willing to tolerate the occasional hole in his glove for the reliable heat of his bat. Accumulating the third highest lifetime minor league batting average (.366), six times leading his circuits in hitting—including the PCL again in 1938 (.350) during a split season with Hollywood and Oakland—Jolley retired from the game in 1941 at age thirty-nine. His final season with Spokane and Vancouver of the Western International League looked like most of the others: 128 RBIs and a .345 batting average, both tops in the league.

As potent as were the Seals' outfields that featured Jolley—none more so than his partnership with future Hall of Famer Earl Averill (.354, 36 homers, 173 RBIs) and Roy Johnson (.360, 20 homers) in 1928—they had their rivals throughout the PCL during the 1920s. The Coast League

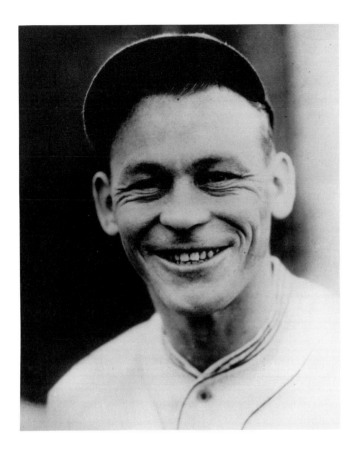

Roy Johnson, a member of San Francisco's celebrated outfield, batted .360 and smacked twenty home runs in the Seals' championship season in 1928. (National Baseball Library and Archive, Cooperstown, N.Y.)

seemed to specialize not only in producing heavy-hitting outfielders but also in gathering them in the same pastures. Like Jolley and his fellow flycatchers in 1928, they were often the keys to pennant-winning efforts. Ross "Brick" Eldred (.351, 71 doubles, 131 RBIs), Ray Rohwer (.325, 33 homers, 155 RBIs), and Jim Welsh (.342), for example, paced Seattle to its only title of the decade in 1924, a slim 1½-game margin of victory over runners-up Los Angeles and San Francisco. Similarly, the Angels' outfield of Art Jahn (.337, 118 RBIs), Art Weis (.317), and Jigger Statz (.354, 291 hits) led L.A. to 121 wins and a pennant in 1926.

Perhaps the strongest outfield combination of the period roamed the distant grasses for the Missions in 1929. Triple Crown winner Ike Boone (.407, 55 homers, 218 RBIs), Irwin "Fuzzy" Hufft (.379, 39, 187), and Pete Scott (.335) contributed to a spectacular .319 team batting average and the best regular season record in the league (123-78). Unfortunately for the Missions, their bats boosted the club to such a commanding lead early in the season that the league owners decided to split the season to stimulate interest in the pennant race. The Hollywood Stars edged the Missions for the second-half title and then won the play-off four games to two on the strength of their own formidable outfield: Elias Funk (.384,

Along with San Francisco Missions teammates Irwin "Fuzzy" Hufft and Pete Scott, outfielder Ike Boone helped to establish a .319 team batting average for the best regular season record in the PCL in 1929. (San Francisco History Room, San Francisco Public Libarary.)

13 homers, 125 RBIs), Cleo Carlyle (.347, 20, 136), and, returned to grace at age thirty-seven with a pardon for his involvement in the post–World War I gambling scandals, Bill Rumler (.386, 26, 120).

Ironically, with all this power at the plate, the hero of the championship series was a pitcher. Ordinary neither on the mound nor at bat, Frank Shellenback surprised very few with a performance that was fairly routine for him. In the midst of a nineteen-year PCL career that had begun with Vernon in 1920, "Shelly" was among a handful of minor league pitchers who continued to throw the spitter after its ban. In 1929 he led the league with twenty-six wins, his second of four twenty-plus-

Hollywood Stars spitball pitcher Frank Shellenback not only led the league in 1929 with twenty-six wins but maintained a .322 batting average, including twelve home runs in regular season play. (National Baseball Library and Archive, Cooperstown, N.Y.)

win seasons between 1928 and 1932. He added two more wins in the play-off but helped his club just as much by sending pitches the other way. Demonstrating that his .322 batting average and twelve home runs in the regular season were no fluke, the PCL's eventual lifetime leader in pitching victories (295) belted a homer in each of the play-off games he won and added another on a pinch-hit appearance in the ninth inning of a game that the Stars eventually took in extra innings.

Across the Bay and away from the San Francisco clubs for which Averill, Jolley, and Boone starred during their relatively few PCL seasons was a player whose versatility and durability made him the league's most dominant player throughout the entire decade. He was the mightiest Oak of them all: Russell "Buzz" Arlett. Emerging from semipro ball at age nineteen with a blazing fastball and a wicked spitter, Arlett showed up uninvited at Oakland's preseason camp at Boyes Springs in 1918. With military service claiming several players from their roster, the Oaks gave the kid a chance to show his stuff. He mowed down the veterans in

The mightiest Oak of them all, Russell "Buzz" Arlett, poses in front of his admiring fans on "Buzz Arlett Day" at the Oakland ballpark, 1927. (Photograph by Moses Cohen. The Oakland Museum Collection.)

an intrasquad game and earned a spot on the team. In the war-shortened season to come, he posted a 4-9 record and a respectable 2.71 ERA.

For the next four years Arlett was the mainstay of the Oaks' pitching staff, notching 95 wins against 71 losses and leading the league twice in innings pitched (427 in 1920; 374 in 1922) and once in victories (29 in 1920). Impressively agile at six-foot-three and 225 pounds, Arlett fielded his position extremely well. Moreover, he also ran the bases well, something that became more noticeable the more he reached base. In 1923 the Oaks took a page out of Babe Ruth's book and inserted Arlett's switch-hitting bat in the lineup on days when he was not pitching. Buzz responded with a .330 average, 19 home runs, and 101 RBIs in 149 games.

The bat used by Buzz Arlett, ca. 1920. Note the misspelling of Arlett's name. (Photograph by Doug McWilliams. Dick Dobbins Collection.)

Like Ruth, who had a remarkable 1919 season after being converted to an everyday player in the outfield, Arlett had turned a corner in his career. For the rest of the decade he pounded PCL pitching at a .357 clip, averaging 54 doubles, 31 home runs, and 142 RBIs per season. Described by a local sportswriter as being "built on heroic lines . . . [and] handsome as most male movie stars are supposed to be and aren't," Arlett was adored by his Oakland fans for his work on the field and his carefree, generous manner away from it.[8]

Like Jolley and Boone before him, and "Moose" Clabaugh and many others after, Arlett suffered bad press because of his fielding. Never as comfortable in the outfield as he had been on the mound, Buzz irritated his critics with a casual approach to his work that suggested the lack of an appropriate major league attitude. However, the offensive numbers he kept posting for the Oaks could not be ignored, and finally, at age thirty-two, he got his shot at the majors. The Philadelphia Phils purchased his contract for the 1931 season and assigned him to right field. Although he started off well, injuries and age frustrated Arlett in his rookie year and he was relegated to a pinch-hitting role by year's end. Still, the big man hit for a .313 average, including 18 home runs and 72 RBIs in 121 games. His .538 slugging average was fifth best in the National League. But 10 errors in 94 games in the outfield revived concerns about his defensive skills and the Phils did not renew his contract. Returning to the minors, initially with Baltimore of the International League, where he twice hit 4 home runs in a game in 1932, Arlett enjoyed several more good seasons in Triple A and Double A ball before retiring in 1937. Fifteen consecutive seasons batting above .300 produced a lifetime minor league batting average of .341. Among his 432 career home runs and 1,786 RBIs were the all-time marks for these categories in the PCL (251

Baseball Cards

In 1909, Obak Cigarettes issued a series of PCL cards highlighting players from Oakland, Portland, Sacramento, San Francisco, Vernon, and Los Angeles. The series continued in 1910, and in 1912 players from the Pacific Northwest League were added. In 1911, the Pacific Coast Biscuit company issued a black-and-white set featuring twelve players from each of the six teams in the PCL, following with a color set in 1912. The infamous and long-running Zeenuts card series depicting PCL players between 1911 and 1938 was the most comprehensive, with nearly four thousand cards issued by the Collins-McCarthy Candy Company of San Francisco. Each card, packaged with one of the company's three candy products (Zeenuts, Home Run Kisses, and Ruf-Neks), came with a detachable coupon redeemable for baseball equipment and other prizes.

In 1928, the Exhibit Supply Company of Chicago issued a black-and-white card set consisting of thirty-two PCL stars. Between 1946 and 1950, local bread companies got into the card-producing business, as Sunbeam and Remar put together a series highlighting the Sacramento Solons and the Oakland Oaks, respectively. The oil companies also got into the act, with Signal Oil assembling a unique postcard-size series of sketches of PCL players in 1947 and Union Oil issuing colored sets in 1947 and 1960 (the latter set devoted to the Seattle Rainiers). In 1949, Bowman Baseball issued the only set not included as a product promotion: a thirty-six-card set highlighting the stars of the PCL.

Given the age of these Coast League cards, the limited distribution, and the occasional cry of "I can't believe my mom threw them away!"—not to mention the attachment of PCL fans to such collectibles—you may not see too many of these baseball cards for sale.

and 1,188). In 1984 the Society for American Baseball Research voted Arlett the outstanding player in minor league history.

Less conspicuous than Arlett's fielding problems were important changes in the business relationships between the minor and major leagues that contributed to his long tenure in the Pacific Coast League. As part of the National Agreement that had been in effect since 1903, the minor leagues accepted a cap on the price of their players who were drafted each year by either major league clubs or teams in higher classification minor leagues. That price had reached $2,500 in 1911 and then remained unchanged through the war years. After the 1918 season, though, as organized baseball on all levels struggled to reestablish itself, the National Association of minor league clubs withdrew from the National Agreement and the draft was suspended. Facing escalating prices for minor league players, the major leagues hoped to reinstate the draft and offered to increase the premium price for draft picks to $5,000. However, the top minor leagues, including the International League, the American Association, and the Pacific Coast League, preferred not to participate in any draft system. They figured that the majors would be willing to spend a lot more than the draft cap for the kind of talent coming out of their organizations.

Strong evidence suggested they were right. After the 1922 season, two stars of the Seals' championship team, center fielder Jimmy O'Connell and third baseman Willie Kamm, commanded offers that had dollar signs spinning in the eyes of the PCL owners. The New York Giants purchased O'Connell for $75,000; the White Sox spent $100,000 to obtain Kamm. Although Kamm enjoyed a respectable major league career, compiling a .281 batting average in thirteen American League seasons, O'Connell was a bust. He played just two years with the Giants before he was banned for life from the game for offering Phillies shortstop Heinie Sand $500 in 1924 to throw a game.

Despite the mixed return on their investment in these cases, the major league owners continued to gamble huge sums on PCL talent. The Athletics' Connie Mack purchased thirty-one-year-old Paul Strand from Salt Lake City in 1924 for $70,000. The Seals sold Paul Waner and shortstop Hal Rhyne to Pittsburgh in 1925 for a combined price of $100,000. In 1927, Portland received from the White Sox a package of players and cash worth over $100,000 for shortstop Billy Cissel. The Oaks sold the double-play combination of their 1927 championship season, shortstop Lyn Lary and second baseman Jimmy Reese, to the Yankees in another $100,000 deal. The dubious knock on his fielding notwithstanding, the principal reason Buzz Arlett stayed in the PCL so long was that, given the kind of money available, the Oaks' owners refused to sell him for any sum less than the six figures they thought he was worth.

With only the sky seeming to be the limit for record-breaking performances on the playing fields and the precedent-setting transactions at the negotiating tables, it was altogether fitting that the Pacific Coast League should pioneer an ascent of a different kind before the 1920s ended. On Sunday, July 15, 1928, the Hollywood Stars became the first professional baseball club to travel by air. Concluding a long doubleheader against Seattle that afternoon, owner Bill Lane and the fourteen members of the Stars' entourage who had not been sent on by rail after the previous day's game flew on a chartered plane to Portland to catch a southbound train, the Cascade Limited, for Los Angeles and a Tuesday playing date. Although it would be many years before such flights became commonplace, once they did the geographical barrier that ensured the hegemony of the PCL over professional baseball in the West soon collapsed. In 1928, however, most viewed the Hollywood team's flight as an oddity, not as a harbinger of a changing baseball world on the wings of a transportation revolution. Secure in its regional preeminence, confi-

Oakland Oaks second baseman James Reese demonstrates his fielding skills at the Emeryville ballpark, 1929. (Photograph by Moses Cohen. The Oakland Museum Collection.)

dent in its product, and comfortable with its profits, the Pacific Coast League anticipated that the good times would keep rolling into another decade even as a deepening national depression began to disrupt the western economy.

Notes

1. Quoted in Polakoff et al., *Generations of Americans,* 601.
2. Quoted in Crepeau, *Baseball,* 6.
3. Sanborn, *The Spalding Guide* (1920), 161.
4. Quoted in Hall, "Scandals and Controversies," 435.
5. Quoted in Asinof, *Eight Men Out,* 172–73.
6. Chicago *Tribune,* Aug. 3, 1921.
7. The original transcript of the Hooper interview cited in Ritter, *The Glory of Their Times,* is in the Hooper Papers, Baytown, Tex.
8. Quoted in Tomlinson, "A Minor-League Legend," 13–14.

4

Austerity in the Thirties

On October 25, 1930, a year and a day after "Black Thursday," a day that capped nearly a week-long frenzy of selling that brought the American stock market to the brink of collapse and the nation to the onset of the Great Depression, the Oakland Oaks hosted a touring team of major league all-stars at their Emeryville home. Taking the mound for the visitors was "Lefty" Grove, whose 28-5 record, 2.54 ERA, and 209 strikeouts for the new World Series champion Philadelphia Athletics had led the majors in all these categories. Adding punch to the all-star lineup was the Bay Area's own Harry Heilmann, who had led his new club, the Cincinnati Reds, in batting with a .333 average after spending fifteen seasons with Detroit. The stars of the Oaks, who had struggled to a fifth-place finish in the recently completed Coast League season, well behind the pennant winners from Hollywood, were two local boys, Buzz Arlett and Ernie Lombardi. Arlett had manufactured another routinely brilliant year, batting .361, belting 31 homers, and driving in 143 runs—his third consecutive season hitting over .360. Lombardi had done better. With a performance as impressive as his proboscis, the twenty-two-year-old veteran of five PCL seasons pounded the league's pitching for a .370 average, his third straight year hitting over .365.

Contributing to their team's victory over the major leagues' best with a couple of hits each, Buzz and "The Schnozz" brought their bats and nicknames to the eastern show the following year. It was a short stay for Arlett, a Hall of Fame trip for Lombardi. Despite leaden feet (8 career stolen bases in 1,853 games), Ernie compiled a .306 average over seventeen National League seasons. Wielding the heaviest bat in the majors, whipping it effortlessly with his huge, interlocked hands, he consistently smashed line drives past the deeply positioned infields he faced, capping an MVP year in 1938 with a .342 mark. When he again led the NL in batting in 1942 (.330), Lombardi became the only major league catcher to win two batting titles. Concluding his career in the majors with the Giants in 1947, Ernie returned to the PCL, where, as one of Casey Sten-

Oakland Oaks catcher Ernie Lombardi poses at the Emeryville ballpark in 1930. (Photograph by Moses Cohen. The Oakland Museum Collection.)

gel's "Nine Old Men" (Lombardi was now forty), he shared the catching chores with thirty-five-year-old Billy Raimondi and in 1948 helped Oakland win its first pennant in twenty-one years.

Whether defeating major league teams on tour, dispatching future Hall of Famers to the bigs (Lefty Gomez immediately preceded Lombardi when the Yankees spent $35,000 pre-Depression dollars to get him from the Seals after the 1929 season), or demolishing the PCL record books (Earl Sheely's .403 batting average in 1930 marked the third consecutive year that the league champion hit over .400), the PCL seemed as healthy as any American institution, well prepared, as the new decade began, to weather tough times. There was no mistaking, however, the threats to the league's—and the nation's—prosperity that the deteriorating conditions of a deepening economic depression brought.

From 1929 to 1933 the national unemployment rate soared from 3.2 percent of the labor force to 24.9 percent. Unable to collect on debts from borrowers who were victims of this displacement, over five thousand banks failed in the country between 1930 and 1932; in 1931 they were closing at the rate of two hundred a month. All elements of the national economy suffered. Farm prices dropped from an index of 100 in 1929 to 44 in 1932, with the average annual net farm income declining from $962 to $288. Business failures, like farm foreclosures, doubled during this brief period, surpassing one hundred thousand. Corporate profits, which had been about $10 billion in 1929, dropped to $7 billion in 1930, $3 billion in 1931, and then disappeared altogether as a deficit of $1.3 billion was reported in 1933. Average manufacturing wages fell 60 percent; average nonagricultural salaries overall fell by 40 percent. Despite President Herbert Hoover's campaign prediction that poverty would be abolished in America and his wishful announcements from time to time that the worst had passed, the mushrooming appearance of shack settlements around the nation's cities, many derisively calling themselves "Hooverville," was eloquent testimony to the depth and cynicism of the suffering.

The facts behind these figures effected the most serious crisis in orga-

Demonstrating the deepening depression of the 1930s on the West Coast, temporary housing was set up in drainage pipes on Oakland's waterfront. This community was given the name "Pipe City" by local residents. Oakland, California, ca.1931. (Photograph by Moses Cohen. The Oakland Museum Collection.)

nized baseball since the damaging sequence during the teens of the Federal League challenge, the interruptions of World War I, and the Black Sox scandal. The decline in recreational spending took a heavy toll at the gate. Attendance at major league parks, which had risen steadily through the 1920s, peaking at 10.1 million in 1930, fell off sharply to 8.3 million in 1931 and bottomed out at 6.3 million two seasons later. The empty seats compelled owners to adopt familiar cost-cutting measures: total annual spending on player salaries in the majors fell 25 percent, from $4 million in 1929 to $3 million in 1933; individual salaries declined on average from $7,500 to $6,000 over the same period. Because they were located in strong markets, some clubs, like the New York and Chicago franchises, weathered these austere years better than most. All, though, tightened their belts and searched for new ways to attract revenues and stay competitive. Many clubs turned to the minor leagues for help.

Top-flight minor league talent, which as recently as 1930 had commanded six figures on the open market, now went for less than half that. Branch Rickey, the general manager of the St. Louis Cardinals, had figured out how to acquire ballplayers even more cheaply. Beginning in the late 1920s, Rickey began to purchase entire minor league teams as a way to ensure the development and flow of players for his major league club. Combined with an elaborate scouting system, this approach brought young talent to an entry level within the Cardinal organization where they could be cultivated for the big club or sold to other franchises. The success of Rickey's "farm" system, underscored in the three National League pennants his Cardinals won between 1930 and 1934, encouraged other major league owners to copy it. The Yankees and the Dodgers especially invested heavily in building large farm systems, although neither was as extensive as Rickey's empire, which by the end of the decade controlled over six hundred players through thirty-three teams.[1]

The majors took more than players out of the minors. They also learned important lessons in the practice of their business. With the number of minor leagues declining from twenty-five in 1929 to sixteen in 1931, the executives of the National Association concluded that bold measures were necessary to save their product. Electing William Bramham, the head of the Piedmont League, its president and granting him wide powers similar to those held by Commissioner Landis, the National Association initiated a series of reforms designed to place minor league baseball on a more solid foundation. Enforcing strict guidelines to drive underfinanced operators from the fold and endorsing modern marketing techniques to promote all aspects of the game, Bramham supervised a national resurgence of minor league ball. By 1940, forty-four leagues, drawing nearly twenty million spectators, operated under the aegis of the National Association.

Underscoring the relative prosperity of the minors during most of the

1930s compared with the slow recovery of the two major leagues was the accessibility of the junior circuits. Offering professional ball at lower cost and greater convenience than that provided by the American and National leagues in the eleven cities in which they operated, the minors also pioneered innovations designed to accommodate the baseball public. Chief among these was the introduction of night games. On April 29, 1930, fully five years before Cincinnati initiated night ball in the majors, Muskogee defeated Independence, Kansas, 13-3, in a Western League game played under the lights at the latter's field.[2] Other minor leagues, including the PCL, quickly illuminated their playing fields. Less than a month after the first night game in Kansas, Sacramento brought baseball under the stars to the West Coast in a game on May 22. Before the end of the 1930 season, six other Coast League teams had either installed lights or announced plans to do so. Ironically, pledging to erect "the best incandescent lighting money can buy" at his namesake ballpark in Los Angeles, Angels owner William Wrigley, Jr., would not offer night ball at the field of his major league club in Chicago for another fifty-eight years.[3]

Distinctions between major and minor league strategies in dealing

A packed house turned out at Wrigley Field in 1939 to watch the hometown Angels play in a night game. (Neg. #15490.2. Los Angeles Daily News Collection, Department of Special Collections, University Research Library, University of California at Los Angeles.)

A view of the crowd at a night game at Seals Stadium in the 1930s. (San Francisco History Room, San Francisco Public Library.)

with the Depression were somewhat irrelevant on the West Coast—after all, the PCL was the major league there. More than ever, the league acknowledged no superior in the quality and exhibition of its product.

Along with Wrigley Field, no place better showcased the PCL's talent or demonstrated the solvency of the league than Seals Stadium. Opening on April 7, 1931, before a packed house of nearly twenty-five thousand, including Ty Cobb, who had traveled from his home in Georgia to participate in the inaugural ceremonies, the new concrete and steel park with the million-dollar price tag was a beauty. An elegant Romanesque façade embraced the single-decked, uncovered grandstand that fully extended down both foul lines. A twenty-foot-high fence, proclaiming on huge advertising panels the merits of the Yellow Pages and various local products, stretched from the left field foul pole to the center field scoreboard. Running along 16th Street in right field to the intersection of Bryant was a bleacher section of fifteen tiered rows of long, backless wooden planks that ended at the three-story combination administration and clubhouse building in the right field corner. A far cry from the rickety confines of old Recreation Park, with its upper deck gambling section, ramshackle wooden clubhouse with only two shower heads in the locker rooms, and chicken wire–enclosed "Booze Cage" where a seventy-five-cent admission charge bought a pre-Prohibition shot of whiskey or two bottles of beer, Seals Stadium now claimed the title "Finest in the West."

In its first season, the new park also housed the finest team in the West—the Seals. Although the spacious dimensions of their new home (365 feet to right, 400 feet to center, 360 feet to left) discouraged the long ball, the Seals featured a lineup of reliable contact men who pounded out the league's highest team batting average (.314). Former Portland star James Keesey, back on the coast after an unsuccessful tryout with the Philadelphia A's, led the San Francisco attack with a .358 average and 113 RBIs. Frankie Crosetti, who would depart at season's end for the majors and a seventeen-year career anchoring the Yankee infield, contributed a .343 batting average, 143 RBIs, and perhaps the best glove in the PCL at shortstop. Henry Kauhane Oana, the Hawaiian "Prince," provided power (23 homers, 161 RBIs) and average (.345) as San Francisco compiled the best regular season record (107-80) and then blanked runner-up Hollywood four games to none in the postseason play-off series.

As much a key to the Seals' success as their steady bats was the strong, sidewinding arm of Sam Gibson. Thirty-two years old and a veteran of three previous minor league circuits, the big (six-foot-two, 198 pounds) North Carolinian had also spent just over three years in the majors, compiling a modest 28-30 record with the American League Tigers and

---

Booze and Betting

San Francisco's venerable Recreation Park, home to the Seals from 1907 until 1930, had two distinctive sections in the park that were unofficially designated the "Booze Cage" and the "Gambling Section." The former consisted of eight rows of benches located under the grandstand, running from just in back of third base, around home plate, to just beyond first base. Only a wire screen separated the spectators from the field, and the bases were only about fifteen feet away. The close proximity to the field allowed opposing players and slumping hometowners to hear the critical cat-calls of those in the cage. Along with the price of admission came either a shot of whiskey, two bottles of beer, or a ham and cheese sandwich. In Prohibition days after 1919, a soft drink was substituted for alcohol, but fans tended to sneak in bootleg spirits to mix with the soft drink.

The upper grandstand section along the first base line was home to the gamblers. Though gambling was illegal, no one interfered with the action and bettors wagered on everything from the game's victor to the outcome of individual pitches.

At its opening in 1931, Seals Stadium was touted as the premier ballpark of the Pacific Coast League. (San Francisco History Room, San Francisco Public Library.)

Yankees, before coming to San Francisco. His Coast League debut immediately established him alongside Hollywood's Shellenback, the Missions' Herman "Old Folks" Pillette, and Tony Freitas of Sacramento as one of the PCL's best hurlers. Like them, Gibson relied on superb control, adequate if not awesome velocity, and thousands of innings of experience. Winning the pitching Triple Crown with a 28-12 record, 204 strikeouts, and a 2.48 ERA, Gibson notched the first of the six twenty-win seasons he would eventually have with the Seals in a PCL career that lasted until 1945. Even then, at age forty-six, Sam was not ready to retire from the game. He bounced around in five more minor leagues before finally calling it quits in 1949 with Griffin of the Class C Georgia-Alabama League. His lifetime totals in the minors (307-200, 3.08 ERA) included 227 Coast League wins.

Not too far from Gibson's stall in the Seals' shared clubhouse was his and every other PCL pitcher's greatest torment in the early 1930s: Oscar "Ox" Eckhardt of the Missions. A natural right-hander who, like Ty Cobb, Harry Hooper, and many others, switched to the left side in the batter's box to gain an extra step down the first base line, Ox had only one year of PCL ball (Seattle, 1929) and two seasons with leagues in his native Texas behind him before settling in with the Missions. He quickly demonstrated the skills that had produced a league-leading .379 average for Beaumont in 1930. Trading power for contact, Ox combined a slashing swing at the plate with a daring manner on the base paths and topped all hitters in his new league with a .369 average. His second consecutive batting title was won with the *lowest* average he would produce in five PCL seasons. From 1932 to 1935, Ox compiled an amazing .392 batting average, three times leading the league in hitting, including .414 in 1933 and .399 in 1935. Both his 1933 season average and four PCL batting titles are all-time league records. Those numbers earned Eckhardt a contract with the Brooklyn Dodgers in 1936, but at age thirty-five he found major league pitching a bit overpowering and finished the season with Indianapolis of the American Association. When Ox finally hung up his spikes in 1940 after a season of Class A ball with Dallas of the Texas League, he owned the second-best lifetime batting average in minor league history: .367. Ironically, the man ahead of him—Ike Boone, with .370—left the Missions for the majors the year before Ox arrived in San Francisco.

The marvelous exploits of Arlett, Lombardi, Crosetti, Gibson, Eckhardt, and Boone underscored the Bay Area's tradition for fielding extraordinary baseball talent. That the cotenancy arrangement at Seals Stadium provided a common showcase for so many of them added to the mystique of the Potrero Hill diamond. It sparkled no more brilliantly than in 1933, when it hosted the rookie season of the lanky, eighteen-year-old son of a local crab fisherman.

Like his older brother Vincent, who had preceded him to the Seals organization in 1931, Joe DiMaggio "preferred almost anything to working on [his] father's fishing boat" and had turned to the rough sandlots of his North Beach neighborhood to escape the docks.[4] He impressed Seals president Charlie Graham well enough with the skills he had acquired there to land a $225-a-month contract for the 1933 season. Initially planning on employing Joe at short, one afternoon early in the season the club's player-manager, Ike Caveney, replaced himself in right field with the young DiMaggio. Unless sidelined with injury, as he was with a severe knee sprain suffered midway through the 1934 season, Joe never missed a game in his new position. In his first season he also never seemed to miss a game without a hit. Beginning with a single off Portland's Art Jacobs on May 28, DiMaggio racked up at least one hit in each of his next sixty games. He was finally stopped, along with all of his teammates, on July 26 when Oakland's Ed Walsh, Jr., no-hit the Seals. Over the course of his record-setting streak, the rookie batted .405,

> **Ox Won the Title**
>
> Any player hitting at a .398 clip might think he had a lock on a PCL batting championship. But in 1935 a young Joe DiMaggio found out that was only good enough for second place, behind Oscar "Ox" Eckhart of the Mission Reds, who led the league with a .399 average. Ox and Joe both took their batting prowess to New York in the 1936 season, with Joe going to the Yankees and Ox to the Dodgers.

Oakland Oaks pitcher Ed Walsh, Jr., ended DiMaggio's streak by holding him hitless on July 26, 1933. (Photograph by Moses Cohen. The Oakland Museum Collection.)

The Streak

Joe DiMaggio's fifty-six-game hitting streak in 1941 with the New York Yankees is well chronicled, but it wasn't his best effort. In 1933, while playing for the San Francisco Seals, the youngster whose name was usually misspelled ("De" instead of "Di") hit in a PCL record sixty-one consecutive games.

The streak began in the second game of a doubleheader on May 28. On July 15 Joe hit in his fiftieth straight game, and the San Francisco *Chronicle* reported: "DeMaggio, 18 year-old batting sensation of the coast League, either has nerves of steel or he has not nerves at all, for the kid slammed out a single in the first inning of the game last night. That hit drove in two runs and smashed the record of forty-nine games made by Jack Ness eighteen years ago."

DiMaggio's streak nearly came to an end in game 60, against Sacramento. Going hitless into the ninth inning, Joe rapped a grounder to deep short, which Solon shortstop Ray French could not handle. Much to the dismay of many Sacramento fans, the scorer ruled it an infield hit. The following day, the *Chronicle* reported: "Police protect scorer who gave Seal youth hit in 60th straight. Questionable safety causes near riot." When the streak finally did end, on July 26 against the cross-Bay rival Oakland Oaks, Joe went out a winner. Although Harlin Pool caught the ninth-inning shot to right field off an Ed Walsh, Jr., fastball, it was hit deeply enough to score Jack Fenton from third base and win the game.

A humble and soft-spoken Joe had never bothered to correct the misspelling of his name in all the newspaper headlines and box scores during the streak, but now that it was over, he pointed out the error so that the watch given to him by the PCL would be engraved correctly.

---

attracted huge crowds to the Seals' games, and earned comparisons with Shoeless Joe Jackson for the fluid quality of his swing. DiMaggio completed his first PCL season with a .340 average, 28 home runs, and 169 RBIs. Two years later, his swing even sweeter under the tutelage of Seals manager Lefty O'Doul, Joe took a .361 PCL career batting average and a "can't miss" tag to the majors for thirteen Hall of Fame years in Yankee pinstripes.

Despite the outstanding individual performances of the players on their clubs, the Bay Area teams only managed one Coast League championship among them from 1932 until 1943. The lone pennant winner during these years was the Gibson and DiMaggio–led Seals of 1935. Sam posted 22 wins in 26 decisions; Joe highlighted an MVP year with a .398 batting average, 34 home runs, and league-leading totals for RBIs (154), runs scored (173), and triples (18). San Francisco frustrated the L.A. Angels' bid for a third consecutive PCL title, defeating them four games to two in the postseason play-offs.

Bracketing the Seals' mid-decade flag was the dominant play of teams

Austerity
in the
Thirties

Joe DiMaggio, of the San Francisco Seals, and Vince DiMaggio, of the Hollywood Stars, are bookends for their family in this 1934 portrait. (San Francisco Public Library.)

to the north and south. Portland ended a long drought of losing campaigns (thirteen in fifteen seasons since the club's last pennant in 1914) with a strong third-place showing in 1931 and then parlayed that awakening to a championship in 1932. Future Boston Red Sox all-star third baseman and manager Pinky Higgins (.326, 33 homers, 132 RBIs), Lou Finney (.351), and John Monroe (.328) keyed a lineup that produced the league's highest team batting average. Although the Beavers crashed to the cellar in 1934, they rebounded for another title in 1936. Nipping both San Diego and Oakland in the season-long standings by a game and a half, Portland defeated Seattle and the Oaks in the play-offs, the first played in the PCL under the Shaughnessy Plan, which pitted the first- and fourth-place finishers in the regular season against each other, while the second- and third-place finishers battled. The winners of the first play-off round then met in the championship series. Veterans Moose Clabaugh (.317, 20 homers, 112 RBIs) and John Frederick (.352, 103 RBIs) steadied the batting order and George Caster (25-13) and Bill Posedel (20-10) did the same for the pitching rotation as the club completed a Cinderella year.

Perhaps the most surprising championship of the thirties, though, was Sacramento's victory in 1937. The Solons traced their PCL roots to the founding of the league in 1903, but, alone among the original Coast League teams, had not yet captured a pennant. They had come close in 1928, winning the second half of the season by defeating the Seals in a play-off, but then fell to San Francisco, four games to two, in the title se-

Sacramento's Solons.
1935.

The 1930s were a rough decade for the Sacramento Solons, who were often a second-division team. In six seasons, including 1935, they finished dead last in the league. (Dick Dobbins Collection.)

ries. More often than not, the Solons were a second-division team. On six occasions, including 1935 and 1936, they finished dead last. But taking heart in the recent success of Portland, the only team in the league with more cellar time than them, the Solons finally lifted the gloom from Edmonds Field and began to string together some strong seasons. The league's only 100-game winner in the 1937 regular season, the Solons settled for less than a full flag, however, when they fell to San Diego in the first round of the play-offs. In the next two seasons they played the role of spoiler, rising from a third-place finish in 1938 and fourth the following year to defeat both L.A. and the Seals for the President's Cup in each play-off series.

Without much punch in their lineup—they trailed the league in team batting in 1938 and 1939—the Solons depended instead on defense and

*Austerity
in the
Thirties*

pitching. No one was more important to this winning formula than a stylish left-hander from Mill Valley, California, named Tony Freitas. Initially breaking into the PCL with Sacramento in 1929, Freitas had successive nineteen-win seasons with the Solons in 1930–31 that caught Connie Mack's attention. The Philadelphia manager brought Freitas to his Athletics midway through the 1932 season, and Freitas delivered twelve wins against only five losses. A relatively high 3.83 ERA, however, which ballooned to 7.27 the next season, sent Freitas packing. Four years later, after disappointing seasons with two American Association clubs and the National League Reds, Freitas returned to the Solons. It was a happy homecoming. Posting a 23-12 mark in 1937, Tony launched six consecutive seasons of at least twenty wins and 290 innings pitched. Continuing to pitch for Sacramento and, after military service in World War II, for Modesto and Stockton of the California League, Freitas completed his playing days in 1953 at age forty-five. He retired with the most wins (342) by a left-hander in minor league history, 228 of them coming in the Pacific Coast League. Similar to its judgment of Buzz Arlett, in 1984

The primary ingredient in the 1938–39 Sacramento Solons winning formula was left-handed pitcher Tony Freitas, who won twenty or more games for six consecutive seasons beginning in 1937. (Photograph by Tommy McDonough. The Oakland Tribune Collection.)

the Society of American Baseball Research named Freitas the minor leagues' all-time best pitcher.

Farther to the north, Seattle emerged from a long somnambulism of its own. Except for 1924, when the "Brick" Elred–led Indians edged Los Angeles and San Francisco for the league title on the last day of the season, the stiff breezes off Puget Sound unfurled no other championship pennants in Seattle's several ballparks. Their home from 1921 to 1932 was Dugdale Park, the second of two fields named after Dan Dugdale, who had played briefly in the National League before moving to Seattle in 1898 as the player-manager of the city's Northwest League team. The ballpark, barren flag poles and all, burned to the ground on July 4, 1932, when an Independence Day fireworks display ignited the wooden stands. Shifting operations to Civic Field, a completely grassless high school sports facility at Republican and Harrison streets, the Indians endured the dust and mud of their "temporary" home through the 1937 season. Their fans suffered no less as the club only managed one winning season and one first-division finish in the thirties. Even that season, 1936, ended on a disappointing note when Seattle dropped four straight games to Portland in the first round of the postseason play-offs.

Brighter seasons and better surroundings were coming. As the 1938 campaign began, newness characterized the entire franchise. The local beer baron Emil Sick, looking to derive a little "fun" from his post-Prohibition profits, had purchased the club during the off-season for $200,000 and immediately had begun construction of a new ballpark for his toy.[5] Erected on the site of Dugdale Park, Sick's Stadium was as elegant a concrete and steel park as Seals and Wrigley and every bit as intimate as Gilmore Field and Lucky Beavers Stadium. With Rainier Avenue running along the first base line and Mt. Rainier rising above the city to the east, the influences on a name change proved irresistible. The Indians were now the Rainiers. In their dugout was a new manager, Jack Lelivelt, who had skippered the Angels for the previous seven and a half seasons. And on their pitching staff was the personification of newness: an eighteen-year-old rookie pitcher directly out of Seattle High School named Fred Hutchinson. These factors combined to effect the most welcome new developments of all in the form of regular season victories and postseason championships.

Beginning with Hutchinson's MVP year in 1938, when he led the PCL in victories (25), winning percentage (.781), and ERA (2.48), Seattle took charge of the Pacific Coast League. Finishing second to Los Angeles in the regular season standings in 1938, despite the club's first 100-win outing since 1925, Seattle began a stretch of six consecutive play-off appearances as the decade ended and another world war loomed. For three straight years, 1939–40–41, the Rainiers entered postseason play as the regular schedule champions. They fell to L.A. in the first round of the play-offs in 1939 but then won the President's Cup three years in a row,

With his post-Prohibition profits, Seattle beer baron Emil Sick purchased the Indians in 1938, renamed them the Rainiers, and immediately built a new concrete and steel ballpark, Sick's Stadium. (Pemco Webster and Stevens Collection, Museum of History and Industry, Seattle, Wash.)

An aerial view of Sick's premier Seattle stadium, ca. 1940. (Photograph by Gordon Williams. UW Neg. #272. Special Collections Division, University of Washington Libraries.)

An interior view of Sick's Stadium, ca. 1940. (UW Neg. #1531. Special Collections Division, University of Washington Libraries.)

The Seattle Rainiers, shown here in 1942, enjoyed six consecutive play-off appearances with three consecutive wins (1940–42). (UW Neg. #11481. Special Collections Division, University of Washington Libraries.)

Considered by many to be the finest team in minor league history, the 1934 Los Angeles Angels won the pennant for the second consecutive year. Even in postseason play, when challenged by a PCL all-star team, the Angels beat the best the league had to offer. (Amateur Athletic Foundation of Los Angeles.)

becoming the first team in the league to accomplish that feat. The third triumph of this streak, in 1942, was especially sweet because the Rainiers rose from third place in the regular season standings to exact revenge on L.A. in the championship round of the play-offs. Dick Gyselman at third, Jo Jo White in center, and Hal Turpin and Tracie "Kewpie Dick" Barrett on the mound underscored the remarkable stability of PCL teams, starring for the Rainiers during each of these pennant-winning years. Both Turpin and Barrett, in fact, had twenty wins or more in each of Seattle's seasons from 1939 to 1942, while Gyselman only missed playing in 9 of Seattle's 530 games over the last three years of this period.

Despite the strong showing of the Seattle teams at the end of the decade and the impressive exploits of individual players like Eckhardt and DiMaggio earlier in it, the 1930s is perhaps best remembered for producing the team that many regard as the greatest in Pacific Coast League history: the 1934 Los Angeles Angels.[6] Deserving a place among such formidable nines in minor league history as the Minneapolis (American Association) Millers of 1910–11, the Fort Worth (Texas League) Panthers and Baltimore (International League) Orioles of the early 1920s, the 1928–31 Rochester (International League) Red Wings, the 1937 Newark (International League) Bears, and the Kansas City (American Association) Blues of 1939–40, the Angels thoroughly dominated their league.

Although losing ace pitchers Dick Ward and Buck Newsom to the Chicago Cubs and St. Louis Browns, respectively, from the pennant-winning cast of 1933, as well as the Cubs-bound bat of Tuck Stainback, Los Angeles immediately signaled in the 1934 season that it was still the team to beat. Twenty-three wins in the club's first twenty-eight games erased any doubts that this would be the case. A 66-18 record at midseason, representing a 19½-game margin over the second-place Missions, eliminated any suspense as far as the outcome of the campaign. Although league officials divided the season at that point to generate some fan interest in the pennant race, the maneuver simply provided the Angels with a new opportunity to demonstrate their prowess. Continuing to win 70 percent of their games in the second half of the season, the Angels finished the year with a 137-50 mark, setting the league's record for team victories in a single season. The Angels also easily established the best winning percentage in league history (.733).

Like every great team in the Pacific Coast League and elsewhere, the Angels featured solid hitting, imposing pitching, and veteran players. Returning from the 1933 pennant winners was the club's entire infield of Jim Oglesby, Jimmy Reese, Gene Lillard, and Carl Dittmar—whose bats contributed to the team's league-leading .299 average and whose gloves were responsible for the circuit's most double plays (212). Fay Thomas (28-4, 2.59 ERA), winner of 22 consecutive games over the course of the 1933–34 seasons, Louis Garland (21-9, 2.67), Emile Meola (20-5, 2.90), J. Millard Campbell (19-15, 2.63), Emmett Nelson (14-5, 2.53), and Roy Henshaw (16-4, 2.75) led the staff, which, not surprisingly, posted the lowest team ERA in the league. Gilly Campbell usually handled the catching chores, adding a .305 bat, 17 home runs, and 97 RBIs to the offense.

As strong as was the Angels' cast within the infield diamond, they had an outfield second to none in the league. Marv Gudat, who had batted .333 for the club in the championship effort of the previous year, played every game in left in 1934, batting .319 and driving in 125 runs. He would add three more .300-plus seasons with Los Angeles before moving on to Oakland in 1938 and eventually completing a twenty-year minor league career, thirteen of which were spent in the PCL, with San Diego in 1945.

Marv's counterpart in right field was Frank Demaree, whom the Chicago Cubs had sent to the Angels for further seasoning. Demaree had had a fair year with the Cubs in 1933 when he batted .272 while filling in for the injured Kiki Cuyler. But when the future Hall of Famer returned to the lineup in 1934 to join Babe Herman and Chuck Klein in the Chicago outfield, Demaree faced little playing time and the Cubs felt that his development would be best aided by a year of everyday play in the minors. It was a perfect prescription. Leading the PCL in hitting (.383), home runs (45), and RBIs (173), Demaree earned league MVP honors for his Triple Crown performance. The Cubs quickly decided that they could find some room for him in their lineup. Frank responded with solid seasons in 1936 (.350, 93 RBIs) and 1937 (.324, 104), each year earning the starting assignment in center field for the National League all-stars. His output fell off quickly after that, however, and in the early 1940s Demaree completed a twelve-year major league career as a journeyman reserve. His last hurrah as a player came in 1945 when he returned to the West Coast and batted .304 for that year's pennant-winning Portland Beavers.

The player who best represented the Angels and their string of twelve consecutive nonlosing seasons from 1929 to 1940, including three PCL titles and three second-place finishes, was Arnold "Jigger" Statz, a feisty speed merchant and fence climber who patrolled the grass between Gudat and Demaree. Graduating directly from Holy Cross College to the New York Giants in 1919, Statz batted .300 in twenty-one games for John McGraw's club but failed to stroke the ball as well in the early going the next season. The Giants traded Jigger to the Red Sox, who quickly dispatched him to the Angels for more work. Statz returned to the majors on two subsequent occasions, providing respectable play (.295 batting average) for the Cubs during three-plus seasons from 1922 to 1925 and spending two less successful years (.264) with the Dodgers in 1927–28. Despite excellent defensive skills, good speed, and a lively bat, Jigger generated little power at the plate from his five-foot-seven, 150-pound frame. That weakness kept sending him back to Los Angeles. When he put on an Angels uniform for a third time in 1929, it stuck. Adding fourteen more years to the four he had previously spent with the club, Jigger established many of the league's longevity records (2,790 games; 1,996 runs scored; 3,356 hits; 595 doubles; 137 triples) before his retirement in 1942, at age forty-five, with a lifetime PCL batting average of .315. Together with his 683 games in the majors, Jigger amassed 3,473 games played in organized baseball, a total surpassed only by Hank Aaron and Pete Rose. His eighteen years with the same minor league club is a record that probably will never be broken.

Jigger's .324 batting average in 1934, his sixth consecutive .300-plus season with the Angels since rejoining them, and his career-best 61 stolen bases provided Los Angeles with an ideal leadoff man in their lineup. His numbers signaled the strength of the rest of the order as surely as did Carl Dittmar's .294 batting average and 73 RBIs from the eighth spot. Finishing the season with 36 more victories than anyone else in the circuit over the course of the entire season, Jigger and company convinced league officials that an ordinary play-off would be a pointless exercise. Instead, the league concocted a series pitting the

In 1932, *The Sporting News* selected Los Angeles Angels centerfielder Arnold "Jigger" Statz the league MVP. Statz went on to set more lifetime records than any other PCL player and later became the Angels' manager. (Neg. #22021.1. Los Angeles Daily News Collection, Department of Special Collections, University Research Library, University of California at Los Angeles.)

Angels against an all-star team drawn from the other PCL clubs. Selected by fan balloting, the all-stars included Eckhardt (.378) and Babe Dahlgren (.302) of the Missions, Hollywood's Jolley (.360) and Fred Haney (.306, 71 stolen bases), Pillette (17-11, 2.60 ERA) and Mike Hunt (.346) of Seattle, and Gibson (21-17, 2.96) and LeRoy Herrmann (27-13) of the Seals. Together, they were no more a match for Los Angeles in the postseason than their respective clubs had been in the regular season. Playing before their proud fans at Wrigley Field, the Angels took the series four games to two and pocketed $210 each for their work. It was a fitting season-ending coup de grace for a team that a visiting Babe Ruth agreed belonged in the bigs.[7]

When many of the 1934 Angels—including Demaree, Thomas, Lillard, Oglesby, and Gilly Campbell—proved the Babe right and headed to the majors over the next two years, the team dropped swiftly in the standings, failing to win a hundred games in 1935 and finishing fifth in 1936 and 1937. But a deeper and, indeed, permanent fall from grace affected their Wrigley Field cotenants. Winning more games between 1930 and 1934 than any other PCL club except Los Angeles, with the likes of Vince DiMaggio, Cleo Carlyle, Dave Barbee, Johnny Bassler, Fred Haney, Archie Campbell, and the indomitable Frank Shellenback, the Hollywood Stars had only the one pennant in 1930 to show for their fine play. After ninety-nine losses in 1935, they lost their identity. With his team drawing fewer than ninety thousand paying customers to its games and facing a 100-percent rent hike for the use of Wrigley the next season, Bill Lane decided it was time to look for greener pastures. On February 1, 1936, the Pacific Coast League approved its first franchise move in eleven years and the Sheiks headed south to San Diego.[8]

Although some league officials doubted that San Diego could support a PCL franchise, the border city of nearly two hundred thousand had a long baseball history that dated to the 1870s when its population barely totaled two thousand. The early clubs in the town, bearing such names as the Lone Stars, the Old San Diegans, and the Young Americans, first competed on a vacant lot at Lockling Square, the downtown intersection of Broadway, Sixth, and Seventh streets. By the turn of the century, additional diamonds appeared throughout the city, as well as sites at Point Loma and Coronado Beach, accommodating a lively baseball scene. The principal playing field was at Bay View Park, located at Logan Avenue and Beardsley (now South 22nd) Street. Hosting both intratown clubs and a series of semipro winter leagues, which, from November to March,

Nicknames

Alan "Two Gun" Gettel, Tracie "Kewpie Dick" Barrett, Ernie "Bocce" Lombardi (most players did not refer to the big and strong catcher as "The Schnozz"), "Sad" Sam Gibson, George "Catfish" Metkovich, "Lucky" Jack Lohrke, "Lefty" O'Doul, Henry "Cotton" Pippen, "Frenchy" Uhalt, "Doc" Newton, "Ox" Eckhardt, "Spider" Baum, "Jigger" Statz, George "Highpockets" Kelly, "Gabby" Stewart, "Ping" Bodie, "Wahoo" Sam Crawford and Carlos "The Comet" Bernier were some of the more colorfully monikered players in the Pacific Coast League.

Runs,

Hits,

and

an Era

served to develop local talent and display the professionals honing their skills, Bay View often attracted several thousand spectators to important games. One of the most memorable occurred on March 3, 1901, when Dummy Taylor pitched his San Diego club to a 1-0 victory over San Bernardino. The low-scoring game was particularly noteworthy because neither team made an error. With typical small-town pride, a San Diego newspaper hailed the event as "the greatest game on record" at the time.[9]

Lacking a ballpark that met league standards, however, San Diego had already failed twice to land an entry in the Coast League. The PCL did not offer the city a place in its initial alignment in 1903 and then refused to let the Salt Lake City team resettle there in 1924. Concern about an adequate playing area almost frustrated Lane's attempt to move his club in 1935. But a hastily concluded agreement between San Diego city officials and the Works Progress Administration led to the construction of a new facility on tidelands property along the coastal highway at the foot of Broadway. Opening on March 1, 1936, for the new San Diego Padres' successful debut against the Seattle Rainiers, Lane Field was as idiosyncratic as its namesake. The distance from home plate to the back-

Ted Williams, along with Joe DiMaggio, is considered one of the Pacific Coast League's most famous alumni. In 1936 he joined the San Diego Padres at age seventeen. A year later he helped lead them to their first championship pennant. (National Baseball Library and Archive, Cooperstown, N.Y.)

During their second season in their new ballpark, the 1937 San Diego Padres brought home the league championship. The first-rate outfield was led by Rupert Thompson and a young Ted Williams. (Amateur Athletic Foundation of Los Angeles.)

stop, for example, was only 12 feet, the shortest of any park in professional baseball. Wild pitches and passed balls routinely ricocheted back to the catcher, preventing runners from advancing. The distance from home plate to first was just as unique—87 feet—a rather critical flaw not discovered for several years. Similarly, the fence sign down the right field line indicated the distance was 335 feet when in fact it was only 325.

Nevertheless, home is where the heart is, if not what the architects' plans said, and San Diegans finally had their league franchise. In 1937, they also acquired a PCL championship. Behind the league-leading bat of catcher George Detore (.334), the strong arms of Jim Chaplin (23-15) and Manny Salvo (19-13, 196 strikeouts), and a first-rate outfield led by Rupert Thompson (.326) and eighteen-year-old Ted Williams (.291, 23 homers, 98 RBIs), the Padres swept both Sacramento and Portland to win the postseason play-offs.

The Stars' departure from Hollywood set in motion the only other franchise move the Pacific Coast League would see until 1956. Always the odd team out in the Bay Area, the Mission club had fallen on hard times since its first and only league championship in 1929. The Missions spent the thirties ensconced in the league's second division, emerging

Runs,

Hits,

and

an Era

———

Walter Judnich of the Oakland Oaks was, in Yankee scout Joe Devine's opinion, a better major league prospect than Ted Williams. Photograph ca. 1937. (Dick Dobbins Collection.)

only once in 1934 as a mere footnote to the Angels' runaway victory. Now owned by Herbert Fleishaker, the team was a losing concern. among several other business interests—especially a brewery—that commanded more of his attention. When no buyers stepped forward to keep the club in San Francisco after a last-place finish in 1937, Fleishaker went looking in the southland for a home and a sale. Neither search was particularly successful at first. But leaned on heavily by the league directors, Angels president Dave Fleming reluctantly agreed to lease Wrigley Field for just one season to the transplanted team with the resurrected name Hollywood Stars. After that they would have to find their own facility.

Encountering similar problems in attempting to sell the team, Fleishaker was forced to hold onto the Stars longer than he wished. Yet, despite a seventh-place finish in 1938 and the uncertainty of their future playing grounds, the new Stars appealed to Bob Cobb, the president of the Brown Derby restaurant chain and an avid baseball fan. Connected to the Hollywood film crowd through his actress wife Gail Patrick, Cobb interested a group including Gracie Allen, Gene Autry, Gary Cooper, Bing Crosby, George Raft, Robert Taylor, Cecil B. DeMille, Barbara Stanwyck, and William Powell to back him for the purchase. The club, including its new ballpark under construction near the Farmers Market out on Beverly Boulevard, finally changed hands in December for a reported $50,000.

The Stars opened the 1939 season in Gilmore Stadium, an oval-shaped park designed for football and midget car racing, while the finishing touches were put on adjacent Gilmore Field. As awkward a grounds for baseball as the Los Angeles Coliseum would be for the Dodgers while their permanent home was being built at Chavez Ravine two decades later, Gilmore Stadium had no dugouts (the players sat on benches on the racing track) and a right field so short—270 feet—that any ball hit over it was ruled a double. Less than two months after the start of the season, however, the Stars took the field in their new park and the Hollywood franchise finally had its own home. The Stars lineup for its inaugural season in Gilmore featured Babe Herman, back in the league from which he launched a twelve-year major league stay in 1926, and Frenchy Uhalt, about halfway through his twenty-season career in the PCL.

Both the look and feel of Gilmore were very different from the scene at Wrigley. A single-decked "fireproof" wooden grandstand curved around home plate at Gilmore and stretched two-thirds of the way down both foul lines. Without bleacher seating in the outfield, the park accommodated under twelve thousand spectators, or about eighty-five hundred fewer than Wrigley's concrete-and-steel confines could hold. Although spacious and symmetrical in layout (335 feet to each foul pole, 383 feet to the power alleys in right and left, 407 feet to center), Gilmore placed the fans in close proximity to the action. The backstop screen was only 34 feet from home plate, the grandstands only 24 feet from the first and third base lines. Many a foul pop landed harmlessly among the fans, giving the hitters a compensatory advantage in the big park.

Gilmore Empire

Gilmore Field, an intimate ballpark built in 1939 to house the Hollywood Stars, was financed by one of southern California's early business magnates, the Gilmore family. Originally from Illinois, Arthur Fremont Gilmore brought his family to Los Angeles in 1874 and started a dairy business, through which he was able to buy part of Rancho La Brea, later the site of Gilmore Stadium and Field. With hard work and luck, the Gilmore fortune grew, no more so than in 1903, when Gilmore struck oil while drilling a water well. He brought his son Earl into the oil business, and it was the younger Gilmore who, upon his father's death in 1918, founded Gilmore Petroleum Co., later the Gilmore Oil Co., and then built Red Lion gasoline stations up and down the West Coast. In 1934 Earl Gilmore built the Farmers Market at 3rd and Fairfax, and that same year Gilmore Stadium was built at a cost of $134,000, at first housing midget car racing and college and professional football. Gilmore Field was built in 1939 at a cost to the oil baron of $200,000 and was the Stars' home park until its demolition in 1958.

As Gilmore's viewing environs put spectators on top of the play on the field, they also created a fishbowl effect in the stands. Principal attention there focused on the celebrity shareholders and their friends who frequently attended the games. During the club's lean years—and there were many before a pennant in 1949—the action in the boxes often created more interest than the game itself. Illuminated with a state-of-the-art lighting system, the park provided as bright a showcase for Hollywood royalty as any theater in town. Immediately becoming one of the "in" places in Hollywood to go and be seen, "Friendly

Austerity

in the

Thirties

95

Joe E. Brown catches and Jane Withers bats on opening day at Gilmore Field, home of the Hollywood Stars, 1939. (Neg. #20417.3. Los Angeles Daily News Collection, Department of Special Collections, University Research Library, University of California at Los Angeles.)

Runs,

Hits,

and

an Era

The exterior of Gilmore Field before a Hollywood Stars night game, ca. 1940. (Neg. #20982.1. Los Angeles Daily News Collection, Department of Special Collections, University Research Library, University of California at Los Angeles.)

Gilmore Field" acquired a character unique to the PCL and all of professional baseball.

Drawing over 260,000 fans to its games in 1939, a healthy proportion of the nearly 2.25 million who attended PCL games that year, Gilmore underscored the stability of the league and the appeal of its product. On the eve of another world war, though, the PCL shared with all levels of organized baseball a sense of uncertainty for its future. Although the game's successful weathering of the Depression may have provided some glimpse of that future, it is unlikely that anyone foresaw the full scope of the economic and social developments that were only a few years away. As always, the Pacific Coast League would be both witness and agent to the changing face of baseball.

Notes

1. Zimbalist, *Baseball and Billions,* 108–9.
2. Another professional club that pioneered in night baseball was the Kansas City Monarchs. Having withdrawn from the Negro leagues in 1930 to become an independent, barnstorming team, the Monarchs carried their own lighting with them, mounted on telescoping poles attached to the back of flatbed trucks. The novelty of the lights, as well as the attraction of the team's play, drew spectators to the games and demonstrated the value of night baseball as a marketing tool.
3. Quoted in O'Neal, *The Pacific Coast League,* 58.
4. DiMaggio quoted in Whittingham, *The DiMaggio Albums,* 13.
5. Quoted in O'Neal, *The Pacific Coast League,* 285.
6. Among those holding this view are Schroeder, "The 1934 Los Angeles Angels," 13–16; James, *Historical Baseball Abstract,* 163–67; Blake, *The Minor Leagues,* 234–35; Sullivan, *The Minors,* 215–16.
7. Quoted in Stump, "The Final Innings," 141.
8. On baseball in Hollywood see Beverage, *Hollywood Stars.*
9. Quoted in Benson, *Ballparks of North America,* 360–61.

5

A Game for All Americans

$\mathbf{A}$s the full fury of the Second World War threatened to engulf the
United States, organized baseball once again faced fundamental ques-
tions regarding its place and role in a nation in crisis. Unlike the years
of neutrality before the American entry into World War I, and despite
the opposition of a powerful isolationist lobby, the United States had
steadily moved toward war preparedness between September 1939 and
December 1941. Perhaps the clearest and most troubling sign of this
course, because it affected millions of men directly, was the Selective Service Act of 1940, which required all males between the ages of twenty-
two and thirty-six to register. On October 16, 1940, National Registration
Day, about fifty-seven hundred baseball players throughout the game's
professional ranks joined over sixteen million of their fellow citizens in
placing their names on the rolls of potential military service draftees.
Limitations within the act on the number of men who could actually be
called for service during peacetime and a generous schedule of exemp-
tions for registrants with wives and dependents ensured no immediate
threat to team rosters.

The Pacific Coast League, like the majors and forty other minor
leagues, completed a full season in 1941, enjoying strong attendance
and providing memorable play. Although there were no individual heroics to match the .406 batting average and fifty-six-game consecutive hitting streak of PCL alumni Ted Williams and Joe DiMaggio, respectively,
in the American League, the staging of the Coast League's first mid-sea-
son All-Star Game on July 29 (won by the South, 3-1) and the tightest
pennant race in many years underscored the sound state of PCL ball.

The attack on Pearl Harbor on December 7, 1941, however, raised
grave doubts about the status of the game in 1942. Although the national sporting press generally argued that baseball provided an important diversion during times of stress, even those tied to the game
questioned the appropriateness of a wartime season and its value if
decimated rosters significantly reduced the quality of play on the field.

Responding to an inquiry from Kennesaw Mountain Landis, major league baseball's commissioner, President Franklin D. Roosevelt provided some clarification in the matter. On January 15, 1942, FDR wrote to express his judgment that baseball was "thoroughly worthwhile." Emphasizing both the relatively short time it took to play a game and the low cost of attending one, the president declared that baseball was "a definite recreational asset" that should be continued for the benefit of American morale.[1]

That professional baseball would be played did not mean that normal conditions would prevail. As the war dragged on, it increasingly determined not only who participated in the game but also the circumstances of play, forcing most minor leagues to discontinue schedules and all teams to fill rosters as best they could. Thirty-one minor circuits concluded seasons in 1942, but only nine continued after that. With over four thousand of the professional ballplayers who had registered for the draft in 1940 destined for some service in the military before the war ended, the teams that survived fielded lineups dominated by overage fathers and underage youths, castoffs and rejects, the walking wounded and the temporarily available. Although rosters everywhere were "as full of unknown names as Y.M.C.A. hotel registers" and the quality of play in the majors slipped "somewhere between AA and A" as the war continued, the game lost none of its appeal, acquiring new prestige for its contributions to the war effort and alleged representation of American values.[2] Nothing underscored the symbiotic relationship between baseball and patriotism more than the now routine feature of playing the National Anthem before every game.

Recognizing that the PCL played a role on the West Coast similar to that of the major leagues in the East and Midwest, Lt. Gen. John DeWitt of the 4th Army Command formally granted permission to the league to open its 1942 season in late March. The early months of the first wartime season were deceptively normal. Enlistments and draft calls had not yet begun to drain baseball's manpower pool, and, despite fears of a Japanese invasion, the league offered a full schedule of day and night games. By late summer, however, much of this had changed. Heeding calls to patriotism and deflecting charges of favoritism, players increasingly entered military service or acquired deferments for work in defense plants. In either case, they created holes in the lineups of their teams that were neither easily nor adequately filled. Similarly, a ban on night games throughout the PCL went into effect in late August and lasted through the 1943 season. Threatened with a shortage of customers, the league turned to morning and twilight games to accommodate war workers and to keep the parks active.

Until the return in 1945 of significant numbers of discharged servicemen, PCL clubs struggled along with their professional counterparts across the nation to field competitive, if not stable, lineups. The league lost players to both the war effort and the majors, which desperately plucked the minors' best remaining players to fill their own depleted rosters, including three Coast League MVPs: Sacramento catcher Ray Mueller (1943), Angels slugger Andy Pafko (1944), and Seals pitcher Bob Joyce (1945). Although they avoided such a dramatic concession to the times as Pete Gray, the St. Louis Browns' one-armed outfielder in 1945, PCL clubs clearly reflected the age gap of wartime rosters. For example, the Angels' backup catcher, fifteen-year-old Bill Sarni, fresh out of L.A. High School and eleven years away from becoming a regular for the St. Louis Cardinals, competed on the same field as forty-four-year-old Charlie Root, Hollywood's best pitcher in 1943, who had won twenty-six games for the Chicago Cubs the year that Sarni was born. Senior even to Root was Herman Pillette, who squeezed out three more years with Sacramento before his retirement in 1945 at age forty-nine.

Further concessions to wartime conditions focused on the nature of the game on the field. As in 1917–18, war goods manufacturing priorities and reductions in equipment budgets forced leagues to stretch their resources, in particular using balls of inferior construction and keeping them in play longer. Fans forfeited their "right" to keep balls that were hit into the stands during the war years, and those who dallied in return-

With player rosters reduced during World War II, teams were forced to find younger talent. Fresh out of Los Angeles High School, fifteen-year-old Bill Sarni was picked up by the Angels as a backup catcher. Photograph ca. 1945. (National Baseball Library and Archive, Cooperstown, N.Y.)

Herman Pillette of the Sacramento Solons was one of the many older players who were available during World War II. Pillette retired in 1945 at age forty-nine. (National Baseball Library and Archive, Cooperstown, N.Y.)

ing balls to the field were the objects of boos and patriotic harangues. Perhaps a principal reason why fans attempted to keep these balls, especially those that reached the stands in fair territory, was the relative rarity of such an occasion in the early 1940s. From 1941 to 1946, the PCL home run kings only averaged twenty-four a season. Ted Norbert's twenty for Portland in 1941 was the lowest league-leading total since 1918, and no lower output has led the league since.

The return of the deadball and the marginal quality of many roster regulars gave pitchers a clear advantage during the wartime campaigns. Veteran hurlers Dick Barrett and Hal Turpin of Seattle, the Angels' Ray Prim, Portland's Ad Liska, Tony Freitas of the Solons, and Bob Joyce of the Seals enjoyed stellar seasons during these years. Joyce's thirty-one wins (against eleven defeats) for play-off champion San Francisco in 1945, for example, was the league's best since Jakie May's extraordinary 35-9 mark for Vernon in 1922. No PCL pitcher has since notched as many victories in a season. In fact, only one, Joyce's successor as the chief of the Seals' mounds corps, Larry Jansen, subsequently reached the thirty-win plateau, hurling a 30-6 season for San Francisco the very next year and leading the club to its first regular season pennant since 1935 (its fourth consecutive triumph in the play-off competition). Larry took his overhand curve and outstanding control to the New York Giants in

A Game for all Americans

In 1946, the steller pitching of San Francisco's Larry Jansen, with a record of 30-6 for the season, led the Seals to their first pennant since 1935. (National Baseball Library and Archive, Cooperstown, N.Y.)

1947. A rookie at age twenty-seven, he debuted impressively, leading the league in winning percentage (21-5, .808) and posting ten consecutive complete-game wins over one stretch. Enjoying several more solid seasons in the majors, including twenty-three wins for the National League champions in 1951, Jansen eventually returned to San Francisco as a pitching coach for the transplanted Giants. Among the players he helped develop were future Hall of Famers Juan Marichal and Gaylord Perry.

With the likes of Joyce, Jansen, Tom Seats (25-13 in 1944), and Ray Harrell (20-18 in 1944) leading its pitching staffs through the war years, San Francisco built up a winning momentum that carried into the late 1940s. Guiding the Seals to six consecutive play-off appearances from 1943 through 1948, occasionally taking a swing at the plate or tossing an inning or two on the mound, was the Seals' popular manager, Lefty O'Doul. Hailing from the city's meat-packing Butchertown district south of Market Street, O'Doul had been wooed back to his hometown to revive the sagging fortunes of the Seals after completing his major league career with the Giants in 1934. The immediate success he enjoyed in guiding the club to the 1935 PCL pennant underscored the unique relationship between O'Doul and San Francisco.

The "Man in the Green Suit" and the "City by the Bay" seemed made for each other. Demonstrations of their mutual affection punctuated their long relationship and forged an identity between the two as strong as any ballplayer has had with his community. In the midst of Lefty's MVP year in 1927, for example, eighteen thousand fans turned out at

---

O'Doul and Japan

Baseball was a smorgasborg for Frank "Lefty" O'Doul. Pitcher, hitter, out-fielder, manager, and ambassador were among the titles he could claim. Though he excelled at every level of baseball and was a true crowd favorite, his role as baseball's ambassador to Japan was arguably his most important.

Baseball was introduced in Japan in the 1870s and by 1930 was the country's second most popular sport next to Sumo wrestling. In October 1931, an all-star team including O'Doul took a two-week trek across the Pacific in a Japanese luxury liner to play exhibition games against various Japanese teams. Lefty's teammates included Lou Gehrig, Mickey Cochrane, Lefty Gomez, and Frankie Frisch. The tour attracted over 450,000 fans and was underwritten by publishing mogul Matsutaro Shoriki, who struck up a friendship with O'Doul and joined with him in making the U.S. all-stars' tour in Japan an annual event. Perhaps their greatest year was 1934, when Lefty convinced Babe Ruth to make the trip along with Gehrig, Jimmy Foxx, and Earl Averill. In 1935, Shoriki and O'Doul put together a barnstorming tour of the United States by a Japanese squad. The team was welcomed to California by O'Doul, then manager of the Seals, who invited them to take spring training with his club and participate in a series of of exhibition games.

Political tension and later World War II kept O'Doul away from Japan until 1946, when he traveled on his own to lay a foundation for future Japanese–United States baseball games. He also pushed for the establishment of a farm system in Japan, a goal that was achieved in 1954. His 1949 tour with his Seals club was an important step in the healing process between the wartime rivals. Ironically, Lefty O'Doul died on December 7, 1969. The "Man in the Green Suit" left a legacy in his hometown and across the Pacific in Japan.

Recreation Park for a day in his honor. O'Doul thanked the crowd with a two-hit shutout victory and then tossed dozens of baseballs to the crowd from a perch atop the grandstand roof. His loyalty to the Seals kept him at their helm for seventeen seasons despite managerial offers at the major league level. When he did leave the city, he was just as likely to travel west as east. Starting with a trip after the 1931 season, O'Doul played a significant role in the development of professional baseball in Japan. Making annual trips to that country during the 1930s, Lefty served as a goodwill ambassador of the game and his city. He considered the attack on Pearl Harbor a personal affront, although he would return to Japan several times after the war as a player, batting instructor, and diplomat.

Applying the knowledge that had produced the majors' fourth highest career batting average—.349—O'Doul tutored nearly a generation of Seals in the fine art of hitting a baseball. The three DiMaggio brothers and Joe Marty, Ted Norbert, Ferris Fain, and Gene Woodling were among the Seals who directly benefited from his guidance, although many others, including Ted Williams, attributed their success at the plate to tips from Lefty. Casey Stengel, O'Doul's managerial adversary with the Oaks from 1946 to 1948 before becoming the Yankees' skipper, felt that "that feller out there in Frisco is the best manager there is" and asked, "Why isn't he up there in the majors where he belongs?"[3] Most likely it was because San Francisco and the PCL were where O'Doul was truly meant to be. Regularly earning over thirty-thousand dollars a season to manage the club, a higher salary than most of his major league counterparts, enjoying the good life that his restaurants and other business interests provided, and basking in the attention that his gregarious manner invited, Lefty was in his element by the Golden Gate. A man of many nicknames—"Mayor of Powell Street," "Father of Japanese Baseball," and, reflecting his often unorthodox directions from the dugout, "Marblehead"—none fit him more appropriately than "Mr. San Francisco."

The height of O'Doul's success as the Seals' manager coincided with the resurgent fortunes of the Pacific Coast League and, indeed, all of organized baseball beginning in 1945. The first collective sighs of relief after nearly four years of war were heard with Germany's surrender on May 7, 1945. As players began to return to their former teams and the easing of wartime restrictions on travel and night games restored minor league schedules to their prewar levels (the PCL had reduced its schedules in 1943 and 1944 from the usual 180-plus games to 155 and 169, respectively), fans demonstrated their pent-up desire for the national pastime and filled the ballparks at all levels of the game's organization in numbers that had not been seen in almost fifteen years. Whereas only twelve minor leagues operated in 1945, forty-two opened play one year later; by 1949, the number had grown to fifty-nine. In the majors, attendance climbed to a new high of 10.8 million in 1945 and then leaped

San Francisco Seals manager Lefty O'Doul hugs Japanese movie star Miss Tanaka at Tokyo's Haneda Airport, 1949. (AP/Wide World Photos.)

over 70 percent to 18.5 million for the 1946 season. Exciting pennant races in the major leagues as well as the PCL and other circuits in the late 1940s no doubt affected attendance. Most likely, though, the relief of economic normalcy after the war provided the greatest stimulant at the gate.

Although such elements of the postwar recovery as the increased urbanization and mobility of a rapidly growing national population were felt throughout the country, no region experienced more dramatic change than the West Coast. Between 1940 and 1945, the federal government had poured over $60 billion into the western states, primarily

This 1945 Hollywood Stars program, featuring Gen. Douglas MacArthur on the cover, was dedicated to all the Hollywood players serving in the armed forces. (Photograph by Doug McWilliams. The Oakland Museum Collection.)

for defense. The aircraft, shipbuilding, munitions, and textile industries that had been developed to defeat the Axis provided a foundation for western economic diversification and population sprawl after the war.[4] Similarly, the favorable experience that many men and women had serving in the military on the West Coast convinced a fair number of them to stay. After their discharges, over three hundred thousand service personnel from other parts of the country elected to settle in California alone.[5] Their relocation contributed to a 53 percent increase in California's population from 1940 to 1950, moving the state from eighth to second in size in the nation. Finding jobs in the arenas of the postwar military-industrial complex or those areas of the economy, such as housing, transportation, energy, and agriculture, that supported the postwar boom, the new arrivals contributed to a birth rate two and a half times the state's death rate. Demographics, federal dollars, and such promising new growth industries as electronics and tourism created optimism up and down the Pacific Coast. No less confident in the implications of these developments for their interests were the Coast League owners. Led

Runs,

Hits,

and

an Era

No fan was left without
a view, as this "knot
hole gang" discovered
at Portland's Vaughn
Street Ballpark in 1948.
(#OrHi 54375. Oregon
Historical Society.)

by their president, Clarence "Pants" Rowland, the league magnates felt that the time was right to launch a bold initiative of their own to secure the future of their enterprise.

Buoyed by surging attendance figures and confident in the quality of their product, PCL executives successfully petitioned their minor league counterparts at the National Association's winter meetings in 1945 to support the league's claim for major league status. The principal results of this designation would be an exemption from the major league draft for the PCL and the right to option players to Triple A circuits without losing title to them. Both measures were critical to player development and franchise stability. Moreover, they were essential if the league were to achieve the competitive level of the American and National leagues.

Notwithstanding the logistical and financial challenges that any major league expansion represented, the PCL proposal insisted that all eight of its teams achieve big league status at the same time, thus creating an entirely new third major league, not just elevated status for a few of its clubs. The major league owners particularly focused on this provision of the PCL petition in rejecting it. Conceding that perhaps the Seals and Angels merited consideration for inclusion in the majors, the owners found that the other Coast League clubs fell short of major league standards in one way or another. Except for Wrigley Field, Sick's Stadium, and Seals Stadium, for example, the PCL ballparks did not impress the major league executives as adequate playing grounds for their game. Sacramento, Portland, Seattle, and San Diego did not appear to have the market base to support a major league franchise. So, too, Hollywood and Oakland, traditionally the weaker clubs in two-team regions, raised doubts about their ability to succeed. Rebuffed but not dissuaded from its objective, the PCL marshaled its arguments and evidence for another go at the majors in 1946.

Robust attendance figures throughout the league in 1946 paralleled developments in the majors and revived hopes of achieving big league status. With new owner Paul Fagan pledging to give San Francisco "the best baseball show in the world," the Seals drew 670,563 fans to their grandly refurbished stadium, complete with baseball's first glass backstop, finely uniformed female ushers, and imported turf installed by a Scottish greenskeeper.[6] The turnout established a season record for a minor league baseball team that lasted until 1982. A single seven-game series between San Francisco and the Oaks during that first postwar campaign attracted over 110,000 Bay Area fans by itself, including a league-high 23,603 for one game on July 30. In the southland, both the Angels and the Stars drew over 500,000 fans to their games, challenging the notion that Los Angeles could not sustain two franchises. Altogether, Coast League turnstiles ticked off 3,718,716 admissions. Amazingly, the league drew over 300,000 more fans to its games a year later, setting the National Association season attendance record for an eight-team league

Fans arrive at Edmonds Field to watch the home team Sacramento Solons play the Oakland Oaks in 1949. (Photograph by Tommy McDonough. The Oakland Tribune Collection.)

PCL executives (left to right) Charles Graham, president of the San Francisco Seals, Clarence Rowland, league president, and Victor Ford Collins, Hollywood Stars president, met in Los Angeles on December 4, 1946, to seek recognition of the league as the third major circuit, along with the National and American leagues. They were unsuccessful in their bid. (AP/Wide World Photos.)

with 4,068,432. Five teams, including two with losing records (Seattle and Hollywood), topped the 500,000 mark in attendance in 1947.

Despite the PCL's record crowds and Fagan's insistence that his "big league city" deserved a big league club, the major league owners continued to reject the Coast League's overtures. Instead, they offered mild concessions to the league's independence. At the 1946 winter meetings, the owners agreed that if a major league team were to relocate in a PCL city, that club would have to pay indemnities to both the local team and the league as a whole. Such a move had almost occurred in 1941 when the St. Louis Browns briefly considered resettling in Los Angeles, but the war shelved those plans. The owners' compensation proposal in 1946 added to the unlikelihood of bringing a major league franchise to the West Coast, for the marginal clubs that might have considered a move— the Browns, the Boston Braves, and the Philadelphia Athletics, for example—could not afford the price. When these teams did move, they headed for cities in league territories—Baltimore, Milwaukee, and Kansas City, respectively—that carried a less costly relocation tag.

With barriers erected to frustrate franchise shifts to the West Coast and the major league owners united in their refusal to recognize the PCL as an equal, the prospects of major league ball in the Pacific states seemed quite remote in the late 1940s. Advising his readers to "lay aside the opium pipe and face the facts of . . . baseball life," *Los Angeles Times* writer Al Wolf concluded that fans "might just as well settle back and enjoy what we've got. Besides, it's good fun, the minor league Coast ball. So far as we're concerned, it'll do handsomely until something better comes along, if and when it does."[7]

Wolf was right on all counts, especially the fun of the postwar pennant races of the 1940s. Four different teams—San Francisco, Los Angeles, Oakland, and Hollywood—won pennants between 1946 and 1949, each capping a tightly contested regular season championship with a triumph in the play-offs. The Stars' five-game margin of victory in 1949 and San Francisco's four-game bulge in 1946 were the biggest during these years. The Angels' flag in 1947 came after a one-game play-off victory over the Seals when both teams had ended the season with identical 105-81 records. The Oaks finished just two games ahead of the Seals in 1948. All the pennant winners, except the Angels, ended long droughts in finishing atop the regular season standings. The Seals, of course, led by Jansen and Fain, had not won a regular season title since 1935. Until Fred Haney took over the managerial reins and Irv Noren fashioned an MVP year (.330, 29 homers, 130 RBIs) in 1949, Hollywood had been looking for another banner since 1930. No team, though, had been denied a pennant longer, or earned a more popular triumph when it finally prevailed, than Casey Stengel's 1948 Oakland club.

With few exceptions, the most noteworthy being Billy Martin, a volatile twenty-year-old infielder barely off the sandlots of Berkeley, the

Oaks were a veteran cast of former major leaguers and minor league lifers. Six of the regulars, including catchers Ernie Lombardi and Billy Raimondi, first basemen Nick Etten and Les Scarsella, second baseman Cookie Lavagetto, and ace reliever Floyd Speer, were at least thirty-four years old when the season started. Another three were thirty-two, including outfielder Brooks Holder, who was starting his fourteenth consecutive season in the PCL. Juggling his "Nine Old Men" and distributing the pitching among a staff whose club leader only had thirteen wins, Stengel perfected the managerial style that would characterize his long tenure with the Yankees. In 1948, it brought the Oaks a pennant and the "Old Professor" a ticket to the Bronx. Five straight World Series championships for the Yankees from 1949 to 1953 underscored the wisdom of the system that had brought a little joy to the aging "splinter emporium" in Emeryville.

While the Oaks and Seals battled across the Bay for the 1948 Pacific Coast League pennant, the San Diego Padres were making headlines of a different sort at Lane Field. Since their last appearance in the play-offs in 1942, the Padres had been mired in the league's second division, losing over a hundred games in each of the last three seasons. Moreover, the departure of Max West and his league-leading forty-three home runs and 124 RBIs for Pittsburgh after the 1947 campaign did not help the club's prospects as a new season approached. Rumors were circulating throughout the league, though, that the Padres were contemplating a bold move to strengthen their roster. Ironically, much of the speculation focused on events unfolding far from sunny San Diego in the front offices of the Cleveland Indians.

For several years, the Padres had enjoyed a working relationship with Cleveland, not unlike that of other PCL clubs with major league teams. These arrangements essentially reserved for the allied club the first opportunity to purchase players from its Coast League business partner. A syndicate headed by Bill Veeck had acquired the Indians in 1946 and, now, under his active leadership, sought to revitalize player development throughout the club's organization. Veeck, like Brooklyn's Branch Rickey, focused particular attention on the most untapped source of player talent in the country for the majors: the Negro leagues. Midway through

Martin's Mentors

Two Hall of Famers and a World Series hero provided guidance to young Alfredo Manuel "Billy" Martin in his early baseball career. In the Oaks' 1948 championship year and Billy's first year with the club, Casey Stengel was the manager. Martin is quoted in Phil Pepe's book *Billyball* as saying that Stengel "was the man who would have the greatest influence on my baseball life." The other Hall of Famer was Oakland native Ernie Lombardi, the hard-hitting, slow-footed catcher who taught Billy how to handle the lumber. Straight from pinch-hitting heroics in game 4 of the 1947 World Series, in which he broke up Yankee Bill Bevens's no-hitter through eight and two-thirds innings with a double that led the Dodgers to a 3-2 victory, was Harry "Cookie" Lavagetto. Cookie, another Oakland native, was an infielder and taught Martin the tricks of playing second base.

A Game for all Americans

Actress Esther Williams prepares to toss out the first ball at the Angels' 1949 home opener. (Neg. #45471.1. Los Angeles *Daily News* Collection, Department of Special Collections, University Research Library, University of California at Los Angeles.)

Runs,

Hits,

and

an Era

Oakland Oaks manager Casey Stengel waves to the crowd from his motorcade after the Oaks' PCL championship victory, October 1948. (The Oakland Tribune Collection.)

Trainer Red Adams (left) attends Oaks second baseman Billy Martin, who is being carried off the field by teammates (left to right) Cookie Lavagetto, Lloyd Christopher, and Maurice Van Robays after being spiked during a play at second. Martin required five stitches to close the wound. Oakland, California, 1949. (The Oakland Tribune Collection.)

At the Oaks' San Fernando spring training camp, manager Casey Stengel (center) sings to (left to right) coach Johnny Babich and players Hersch Martin, Vince DiMaggio, and Arkie Biggs, March 1948. (The Oakland Tribune Collection.)

The "Old Professor of Baseball," Casey Stengel stands in front of the 1948 championship team that brought the PCL pennant to Oakland for the first time in twenty-one years. The team, featuring the famous "Nine Old Men," was honored at the Oaks' ballpark by Ed Hogarty, president of the Oakland Boosters. Stengel went on to manage five straight world series championships with the New York Yankees from 1949 to 1953. (The Oakland Tribune Collection.)

New Oaks manager Charlie Dressen does some gentle sparring at the airport with former Oaks manager Casey Stengel. Brick Laws, owner of the Oakland club, monitors the bout, ca. 1949. (The Oakland Museum Collection.)

Oaks stars (left to right) Charley Gassaway, Ralph Buxton, Mickey Burnett, Cotton Pippen, Red Mann, and Gene Bearden are shown here playing cards and kibitzing during the train ride to their 1946 opening game against the San Diego Padres. (Photograph by Tommy McDonough. The Oakland Tribune Collection.)

the 1947 season, while Jackie Robinson was breaking the color line and posting rookie-of-the-year numbers for the Dodgers, Veeck quietly re-cruited twenty-two-year-old Larry Doby from the Newark Eagles to play ball for the Indians. Although Doby struggled that summer in a bit role for Cleveland, he won a starting spot in the Indians' outfield in 1948 and contributed a .301 batting average and sixteen home runs to the club's World Series championship year. Mindful of Robinson's success and confident in Doby's ability, Veeck encouraged the minor league teams associated with the Indians to look to the Negro leagues for new talent. On March 30, 1948, the Padres responded, sending John Ritchey, the 1947 batting champion of the Negro American League, to pinch-hit in a game against Los Angeles. Given the starting assignment as catcher the next day, Ritchey homered and went on to bat a solid .323 for the season.

The segregated conditions in the PCL that the Padres and Ritchey challenged closely paralleled those throughout organized baseball. Since the late 1880s, when racial segregation emerged as a national institution affecting all aspects of American society, baseball too had erected barriers

Former San Diego Padre slugger Max West is pictured in 1951 with his Los Angeles Angels teammate Chuck Connors. While with the Padres in 1947, West led the PCL with forty-three homers and 124 RBIs. Connors was a popular player who went on to a successful television career. (Dick Dobbins Collection.)

to define its distinctiveness and "protect" its respectability. Indeed, the affiliated clubs of the National Agreement underscored their particular culture of professionalism in referring to their operations as "organized" and labeling those beyond their jurisdiction as "outlaws."[8] Although a few black players like George Stovey, Bud Fowler, and Moses Walker continued to play in the International League and other organized circuits through most of the 1880s, the last decade of the nineteenth century dawned without a black player on any National Association roster. After Walker's final season with Newark in 1889, organized baseball would not officially see another black player until Robinson took the field in 1946 for the Montreal Royals of the International League.

With the color line firmly in place, blacks who aspired to play baseball professionally had few outlets available to them. But forming their own teams and leagues, playing winter ball in Cuba, Mexico, or Venezuela, where they were enthusiastically welcomed, or, very rarely, appearing on the groomed fields of the majors or organized minors under pseudonyms or other guises, skilled black ballplayers found alternative means to pursue a living in the game. The Cuban Giants, for example, an all-black team formed among the waiters of the Argyle Hotel in Babylon, New York, embarked on a tour of several eastern states in 1895 that set the tone for the great barnstorming teams of the 1920s and 1930s. Although many of these teams, such as the Kansas City Monarchs, the Homestead Grays, and the Chicago American Giants, also competed in various Negro leagues, those circuits were generally haphazard affairs with shaky franchises and uncertain schedules. Despite its own hazards and unreliable conditions, barnstorming cultivated a black ballplaying fraternity and provided both visibility and competitive respect for the players, particularly on those frequent occasions when they competed successfully against white teams.

Blacks and other players of color on the West Coast exhibited no less an interest in baseball than their counterparts in other regions of the country, nor did they encounter any different obstacles in pursuing the game professionally. Although a few black players, most notably the mulatto catcher Horace Wilds, competed for otherwise all-white amateur and semiprofessional teams in the 1880s, this route was rarely traveled; and after 1888 it was not traveled at all. When the Oakland Tribune club for which he played disbanded in 1888 with the collapse of the short-lived Pacific Baseball League, Wilds shared with Moses Walker the sad distinction of being the last holdouts against the absolute rule of Jim Crow in baseball. Wilds, "the colored beauty," as he was described in one newspaper account, thereafter found only all-black nines eager for his services.[9]

Excluded from the California and Pacific Northwest leagues by the same informal agreement to police the color line that owners and league officials acknowledged nationally, West Coast African Americans formed their own teams. Such clubs as the Cuban Giants and the Quicksteps originated in Los Angeles, while a San Francisco all-black nine calling itself the Darkies added variety to the Bay Area baseball scene. Like the Negro league barnstormers several decades later, California's black clubs of the late nineteenth century impressed spectators with their play. Covering a game between the black employees of San Francisco's Pacific Hotel and the all-black Union club of Oakland, for example, a reporter observed that "the game was a great deal better than some of the championship contests [of the California League] and several brilliant plays were made."[10] Except for an occasional attempt to disguise a player's racial identity in order to smuggle him into a lineup—the Oaks tried to

A
Game
for all
Americans

pass the fair-skinned pitcher Jimmy Claxton as a Native American in 1916 but failed to fool anyone for very long—the Pacific Coast League cooperated fully in the conspiracy against integrated play that united organized baseball.

The player shortages during World War II and the blatant contradictions within the nation's war aims abroad and racial practices at home provided new contexts for baseball to reevaluate its personnel policies. Questioned about the rationality of rosters featuring a one-armed outfielder, a fifteen-year-old catcher, and numerous over-the-hill veterans while established stars from the Negro leagues remained unsigned, a few owners made gestures toward integration. None of these, including aborted tryouts in 1943 for Negro league stars Lou Dials and Chet Brewer with the Angels and Oakland Oaks, amounted to anything. Overruling the offer of a tryout his club's president, Pants Rowland, made to Dials and Brewer, Angels owner Phil Wrigley, the son of William Wrigley, told the players that his team did not have a place for them. Similarly, Oakland's owner, Vic Devincenzi, capitulated to the refusal of his manager, Johnny Vergez, to audition them.[11]

Despite mounting pressures for equal access to all the game's playing fields, a campaign vigorously pursued by such West Coast newspapermen as Hallie Harding of the Los Angeles *Sentinel* and Art Cohn, sports editor of the Oakland *Tribune,* the war years ended with the racial barrier unbreached. Discouraged by the prospects for integration, yet aware that Negro league games had posted solid attendance figures throughout wartime, a few black businessmen gambled that such a league could flourish on the West Coast. Spearheaded by Eddie Harris and several fellow members of Berkeley's all-black High Marine Social Club, the effort culminated in the establishment of the West Coast Baseball Association (WCBA).[12]

The six-franchise circuit, including the Oakland Larks, the San Francisco Sea Lions, the Fresno Tigers, the Portland Rosebuds, the Seattle Steelheads, and the Los Angeles White Sox, opened the season in early May 1946. Playing its games in the rented ballparks of PCL teams when those teams were on the road, and filling its rosters with former Negro leaguers, eastern barnstormers, and local talent, the WCBA got off to a promising start, drawing good fan support. The Larks, for example, attracted over six thousand fans to their "home" opener in Seals Stadium. However, despite a respectable draw of about three thousand fans a game, the league quickly ran into trouble. Victimized by mismanagement and limited finances, it folded that July. Although the Larks remained virtually intact as a barnstorming team after the WCBA's collapse, most players, including future Oakland mayor Lionel Wilson, put their brief professional careers behind them. Whether the league could have survived under different circumstances became moot when Jackie Robinson took the field for Montreal. His debut made the WCBA an anachronism even before its first pitch was thrown.

Just as Robinson's success with the Dodgers and Doby's with the Indians had stimulated other major league clubs to sign black players, Ritchey's fine performance with San Diego during his ground-breaking first season had an immediate effect on PCL rosters. In 1949 the Padres added thirty-four-year-old Luke Easter to their lineup, and the six-foot-four, 240-pound colossus, acclaimed as the "greatest natural hitter the Coast League has seen since Ted Williams," quickly became one of the league's main attractions.[13] In only 80 games with San Diego, Easter belted 25 homers, collected 92 RBIs, and batted .363. Marveling at the prodigious distances he could hit a ball, Sacramento manager Del Baker declared, "I've never seen anybody better than Easter."[14] Hollywood skipper Fred Haney agreed, adding, "I wish they'd get him out of here before he kills every infielder in the Coast League."[15] Cleveland granted Haney's wish, bringing Easter to the majors toward the end of the 1949 season. Although well past his prime, Easter gave the Indians one of the most potent one-two power punches in the majors with his teammate Larry Doby. For the 1950–52 seasons, Luke blasted 86 homers and Larry hit 77.

Also helping the Padres to their first winning season and play-off appearance since 1942 was Orestes "Minnie" Minoso. The "Cuban Comet" had demolished pitching in Class A and Class AA ball with other Cleveland farm teams before coming to San Diego. His quick bat treated the PCL arms just as rudely, hitting .297 with 22 round-trippers. Before heading to the majors, Minoso led the Padres to 114 wins and a second-place finish in 1950 with a .339 average, 20 home runs, 115 RBIs, and 30 stolen bases. Although bound for a less distinguished major league career than Minoso, Harry "Suitcase" Simpson completed his minor league seasoning with the Padres as well, leading the PCL in 1950 with 156 RBIs, slamming 33 home runs, and batting .323.

Prompted by the gate appeal and winning influence of the black Padres, other Pacific Coast League teams quickly scrambled to integrate their rosters. Six years after they snubbed Dials and Brewer, the Angels signed right-hander Booker McDaniels, who posted an 8-9 record for

> **Padre Power**
>
> Left-handed outfielder/first baseman Jack Graham was one of a group of hard hitters who graced the lineup of the San Diego Padres. Max West, Luke Easter, and Graham terrorized Coast League pitchers and sent the ball flying out of Lane Field at a record pace. West led the league in home runs in 1947 (43) and 1949 (48), with Easter contributing 25 in only 80 games in 1949 before being called up to Cleveland. In 1948, Graham, the son of George "Peaches" Graham, a major leaguer between 1902 and 1912, appeared to be on a pace that would allow him to surpass Tony Lazzeri's 1925 record of 60 homers. By July 25, Graham had hit 46 home runs and the *Pacific Coast News* declared: "Graham appears a cinch to break Lazzeri's hitting mark even should he falter in the last two months. At his current pace, the San Diego flyhawk/first baseman will have hit 78 fourbaggers, well over Tony's 60 figure." That very day, in a game against the Angels, Jack was hit on the head by a Red Adams pitch, causing him to miss 51 games and hindering his performance in the games in which he did play. Though Lazzeri's record was safe, Graham finished the season with 48 homers and picked up MVP honors for his gutsy play.

Luke Easter joined the San Diego Padres in 1949 at the age of thirty-four. He was considered the greatest natural hitter the league had seen since Ted Williams. (Dick Dobbins Collection.)

Orestes "Minnie" Minoso, also known as the "Cuban Comet," contributed a .297 batting average and twenty-two home runs to help lead the San Diego Padres to the 1949 play-offs, their first appearance in the championship series in seven years. (National Baseball Library and Archive, Cooperstown, N.Y.)

Artie Wilson slides into home with one of the runs that led the Oaks to an 8-3 victory over the Hollywood Stars in May 1949. Umpire Bill Engeln calls Wilson safe as the ball sails past catcher Jack Paepke. (The Oakland Tribune Collection.)

last-place L.A. in 1949. Sacramento fared better with Bob Boyd, whose line drive hitting netted a .342 batting average in 1951 and the nickname "The Rope." No less darting on the base paths, Boyd led the league with 41 steals before departing for the Chicago White Sox late in his rookie season. Oakland added two black infielders in 1949, Parnell Woods and Artie Wilson. The former disappointed; the latter sparkled.

Rivaling Easter among the PCL's early black pioneers for having the greatest impact on his team and in the league, Wilson had actually begun the 1949 season as Luke's teammate with San Diego. But a dispute between Cleveland and the Yankees regarding the rights to his contract went New York's way, which then dispatched him to Oakland. It was no wonder so many clubs were interested in Wilson. The premier leadoff man and shortstop in the Negro leagues in the 1940s, Artie hit over .371 from 1944 to 1948, leading the Negro American League with a .402 average the last year. Slapping pitches so adroitly to the opposite field that rival managers adopted a special shift to try to contain him, Wilson collected a league-leading 211 hits to win the PCL batting title with a .348 mark. Turning double plays with his infield partner and roommate Billy Martin as skillfully as he hit and ran the bases (he also led the league with 47 steals), the "Birmingham Gentleman" charmed the Oaks' fans with his engaging manner and stellar play. In 1950, he again anchored Oakland's infield, contributed a .314 bat to the best-hitting team in the league, and enjoyed a pennant-winning season.

Despite their success on the field, the first black players in the Pacific Coast League were constantly reminded of the novelty of their presence and the challenges it posed to the prevailing racial attitudes of postwar American society. With rare exceptions—the Artie Wilson–Billy Martin relationship being perhaps the best example—black players suffered a cruel isolation from their teammates. Often denied access to the same hotels and restaurants as the white players, subjected to racial taunting at the ballpark, and aggressively targeted with beanballs and flying spikes by opposing players, they, like Jackie Robinson, kept much of their frustration in check and fought back only with their skillful play—at least initially.

After several seasons of such treatment, the frustrations of the black players finally exploded in a free-swinging melee on July 27, 1952, triggered when Piper Davis of the Oaks bowled over Seals pitcher Bill Boemler on a play at the plate. Boemler had a notorious reputation for headhunting, having plunked Davis and his black teammate Ray Noble earlier in the season. Twice decked by the Seals' pitcher on this day, Davis had doubled his way on base and, with Boemler covering home on the ensuing play, saw his opportunity for revenge as he rounded third. The bench-clearing brawl that followed—"one of the most slambang baseball fights ever witnessed," according to one reporter[16]—spilled over into the stands and raised fears of a full-scale race riot. Although a San Francisco–based contingent calling itself "The Group of 19" promised retaliation to Davis and Noble the next time they played in Seals Stadium, nothing came of the threat.

By contrast, Artie Wilson would recall many years after his playing days with the Oaks that his own experience had been "really nice—no problems whatsoever."[17] Compared to the conditions that black players faced in other parts of the country, particularly in some southern leagues where race baiting and threats of bodily harm were more flagrant, Wilson's assessment was probably quite accurate. Nevertheless, it cannot ignore the record that gaining access to the playing field, in the Coast

League as elsewhere, was only the first step toward equality in the game.

As Ritchey, Easter, Wilson, Minoso, and Davis helped tear down the walls of segregation in the PCL, the league neared the half-century mark of its existence. Its playing fields enriched with the talents of the black players, its games enlivened with a postwar power boom, and its parks enjoying overflow crowds, the Coast League had reaffirmed its position as organized baseball's most successful and prestigious minor league. Still, the designation "minor" continued to irk those who felt that the circuit had earned parity with the National and American leagues. Although the campaign to seek major league status for the PCL had quieted after 1947, its advocates resumed the push in the early 1950s. Little did they anticipate, however, how the league would be transformed over the next decade or the forces that would dictate change throughout all of minor league baseball.

Notes

1. Roosevelt to Landis, Jan. 15, 1942, Landis File, National Baseball Library, Cooperstown, N.Y.

2. *Time* magazine article, 1945, quoted in Lingeman, *Don't You Know There's a War On?,* 312–13.

3. Quoted in Leutzinger, "Historical Perspective: Lefty O'Doul," n.d., clipping in O'Doul File, National Baseball Library, Cooperstown, N.Y.

4. Gibson, *The West,* 580.

5. Rolle, *California,* 567.

6. Quoted in Svanevik and Burgett, "The City's Long Tradition," D3.

7. Wolf, "Coast Deal a Long Way Off," 17–18.

8. Tygiel, *Baseball's Great Experiment,* 14–15.

9. Oakland *Tribune,* Sept. 5, 1887, 3.

10. San Francisco *Chronicle,* June 24, 1889, 7.

11. Cooper, "Breaking the PCL Color Barrier," D-2.

12. Cooper, "West's Short-Lived Black League," E-1, E-3.

13. Quoted in *The Sporting News,* Apr. 20, 1949.

14. Baker quoted in ibid., Oct. 12, 1949.

15. Haney comment in newspaper clipping, n.d., Easter File, National Baseball Library, Cooperstown, N.Y.

16. Quoted in Tygiel, *Baseball's Great Experiment,* 256.

17. Quoted in Cooper, "Breaking the PCL Color Barrier," D-2.

6

Transformation in the Fifties

In an interview with H. G. Salsinger of the Detroit *News* at the start of the 1948 season, Hollywood Stars owner Bob Cobb addressed the issue of major league status for his circuit. The difference between a major and a minor league, he explained, was "size of parks, attendance, prices of admission and players' salaries. That's about all." Notwithstanding the importance of each of these defining characteristics and the factors behind them—franchise population bases, strength of local economies, quality of play, and club finances, for example—Cobb insisted that all the Pacific Coast League needed to "bring our inventories of players up to major league standards and rebuild our parks to major league proportions" was a six-year moratorium on the annual player draft. Not content to focus on the needs of the PCL to match the bigs, he concluded the interview with a critical assessment of the league vis-à-vis other minor leagues. Referring specifically to the American Association and the International League, Cobb pointed out, "We are classed with [them], but we outdraw both. What is more, we pay higher salaries than either. . . . We have a great deal more class."[1]

Although many of Cobb's arguments regarding the strengths of the PCL were valid, his arrogance promised neither to win too many friends for the league nor to influence too many people in supporting its quest for parity with the National and American leagues. Yet, it was hard to ignore the success of the PCL.

Fifty-seven players on the 1948 rosters of the two major leagues came from the PCL. All eight of the PCL managers for the 1951 season were either former major league managers or players or both. Four former PCL skippers had moved in the other direction: Oakland's Stengel to New York and Chuck Dressen to Brooklyn, San Diego's Bucky Harris to Washington, and Seattle's Paul Richards to the White Sox. Rogers Hornsby of the Rainiers joined them a year later when his old club, the Cardinals, named him their pilot. The new black stars and tight pennant races attracted fans to the Coast League ballparks in healthy numbers, although

Hall of Famer Rogers Hornsby is pictured during his single year as coach of the Seattle Rainiers, 1951. (Dick Dobbins Collection.)

attendance figures did not match the consecutive record turnouts of 1946 and 1947. Attempting to capitalize on the popularity of the PCL and promote their own teams, the Angels and the Stars began televising some of their games. Hollywood experimented with the new medium first, in 1947, and Los Angeles followed a year later. By 1949, both clubs were televising most of their home games.

Ironically, if the advent of the television age signaled interest in the league, it did not manifest itself at the gate. As the images on home screens and the national broadcast of a major league game of the week over Mutual Radio entertained fans away from the local parks, PCL attendance fell off 15 percent in 1950 from the year before. The drop was particularly disappointing because the league had expanded its regular season schedule to 200 games, the most since 1930, in an effort to bolster attendance. Abandoning that experiment after just one year, the PCL returned to a schedule that never again exceeded 180 games. Fewer games in 1951, however, meant fewer admissions, and overall league attendance dropped another 30 percent, from 3.1 million to 2.2 million.

The bad news at the turnstiles did not deter Fagan, Cobb, and others from their efforts to elevate the PCL to major league status. That possibility received encouragement when, under the direction of new baseball commissioner Ford Frick, the major league owners approved a unique AAAA classification for the PCL at their 1952 winter meetings. The move essentially ordained the Coast League with an "open" classification, allowing it to set its own player salaries and providing it with some protection from the major league player draft. The designation, however, did not signal that the major leagues would shortly be inviting the PCL to their table as an equal. In fact, it seemed little more than symbolic, for accompanying the Four A tag were strict standards that any team so classified had to meet to merit major league status. These included an aggregate population base of fifteen million in the cities of the teams' league, seating capacity of at least twenty-five thousand in all of the league's ballparks, and total league paid attendance in excess of 3.5 million for each of the previous three years. The PCL only met the first of these three conditions. Never-

---

Fouled Off Again, and Again, and . . .

In the early years of PCL radio broadcasting, stations aired the home games of local teams live from the ballpark. The tricky part was when these stations tried to broadcast road games by recreating them at the station, many miles away from the ballpark. Announcers such as Bud Foster, who worked the Oaks games, would receive a brief description of the action via the telephone or telegraph and would improvise an account of the game as if he were viewing it. He would also be responsible for the "sounds" of the game, slapping his leg to mimic a ball being caught and playing recorded cheers at the appropriate times. A real dilemma would occur when the telegraph or telephone broke down for several minutes and the announcer had to improvise. So as not to distort the action of the game, many announcers would have the last batter before the interruption foul the ball off numerous times until the transmission returned.

Transformation in the Fifties

theless, a new outbreak of major league "fever" had many Coast Leaguers once again contemplating a place in the bigs.

While the meaning of the PCL's new status invited speculation about the league's future, its fans enjoyed the more immediate drama on the diamonds. Early 1950s baseball in the league provided a theatrical tour de force. Heroic performances by Seattle's "Jungle Jim" Rivera (.352, 20 homers, 112 RBIs) in 1951 and Hollywood's Johnny Lindell (24-9, 190 strikeouts) in 1952 earned each of them MVP honors as they led their clubs through pennant-winning campaigns before departing for the majors. Bob Dillinger's league-leading .366 batting average for the Solons in 1953 would not be topped for twenty-six years. Carlos "The Comet" Bernier swiped 65 bases for the Stars in 1952, the most since his manager, Fred Haney, pilfered 71 in 1934 and, like Dillinger's average, an unsurpassed target until 1979. Marks that have not been bettered in the PCL since they were set during these years included the 246 strikeouts Sam Jones recorded for the Padres in 1951 and Red Munger's 1.85 ERA for Hollywood in 1955.

> **Another Hollywood First**
>
> We usually associate cheerleaders with football and basketball, but in 1952 the colorful Hollywood Stars made them part of the game at Gilmore Stadium. Situated atop the dugout or down the outfield lines, decked out in eye-catching uniforms and pompons, the cheerleaders were crowd favorites and devoted to the fates and fortunes of their beloved Stars.

The best ensemble work from 1951 to 1955 occurred at Gilmore Field and Sick's Stadium. Capturing two pennants each during these years, the Stars and the Rainiers posted winning percentages of .576 and .540, respectively, considerably better than San Diego's .517, the only other Pacific Coast League team above the .500 mark for this five-year period. Except for Seattle's fifth-place slump in 1954, neither club otherwise finished lower than third or turned in a losing record. For three consecutive years, 1952–53–54, the Stars won over one hundred games. Only Oakland in 1952 and the Padres in 1954, when they frustrated Hollywood's bid for a third straight flag with a one-game postseason play-off victory, won as many in a single season.

Relying on strong arms—Lindell, Munger, Ben Wade, Art Schallock, Paul Pettit, Jim Walsh, George O'Donnell, Roger Bowman, Lino Dinoso, Mel Queen, and Bob Garber—and a solid offense typified in the successive league MVP performances of Dale Long (.272, 35 homers, 116 RBIs) in 1953 and the clutch-hitting Jack Phillips (.300) in 1954, the Twinks wore the "dynasty" mantle as well as any PCL team for a comparable five-year stretch. They were easily as entertaining and pugnacious as any of their predecessors. The latter quality may partly have been a by-product of Cobb and Haney's decision in 1950 to outfit the team in pinstriped short pants. Borrowing the idea from a visiting British soccer club, whose players impressed the Stars' brain trust with their speed, the owner and manager insisted that exposed legs would allow their men to

Runs,

Hits,

and

an Era

130

move more quickly along the base paths. The innovation had predictable results: fans were shocked, players were embarrassed, and the ridicule was unrelenting. One headline asked, "Will the Stars Shave Their Legs Next?" Another wondered whether their uniform designer was Ginger Rogers. The eastern press labeled the move "bush league" and just another "screwball stunt from Movieland."[2] Closer to home, the Stars suffered suggestive whistles from fans and merciless ragging from their opponents regarding the nature of their manhood. Although the club won eight of its first nine games wearing shorts, Cobb eventu-

Hollywood Stars manager Fred Haney displays his novel idea for a short-panted uniform, which was adopted by the Stars in 1950. Left to right are Fred Haney, Bill Schroeder, Harry Williams (PCL secretary), and a young woman who later became the team's model for their innovative uniforms. (Photograph by H. Lee Hansen. Amateur Athletic Foundation of Los Angeles.)

Always the innovators, the Hollywood Stars were the only team in the Pacific Coast League to have cheerleaders, ca. 1952. (Bob Reiss.)

An angry Billy Schuster, the Angels shortstop, waves his bat at umpire Gordon Ford as Oaks catcher Don Padgett looks on. Schuster was subsequently thrown out of the game. Emeryville, California, 1949. (Photograph by Tommy McDonough. The Oakland Tribune Collection.)

ally heeded his players' pleas for more traditional dress. Thereafter, the shorts only appeared on weekends and holidays, but it took three years before they disappeared completely.

Whether or not the shorts compelled the Stars to demonstrate their virility more aggressively than their conventionally attired counterparts in the league, some of the most notorious brawls and temper tantrums in PCL history involved Hollywood players. On August 2, 1953, for example, the arch rivalry between the Stars and the Angels, which had occasioned a steady diet of unpleasant exchanges between the players of both teams and their fans over the years, finally erupted in a full-scale riot at Gilmore Field. The fight occurred in two stages. First, L.A.'s Joe Hatten, the league leader with 152 strikeouts that season and the pitcher most responsible for the club's first ninety-plus win season since 1948, nailed Hollywood's popular veteran Frank Kelleher with a fastball. The pitch was no accident, for Kelleher had managed six consecutive hits off Hatten before this at bat and the L.A. hurler was clearly frustrated. Kelleher stormed the mound and both players were ejected in the scuffle that followed. That set the stage for round 2. Ted Beard, who had been put in to run for Kelleher, slid hard into the Angels' third baseman, Murray Franklin, on an ensuing play. Both players came up swinging, and their teammates quickly joined in the fray. Unlike most baseball fights where the benches clear and a circle forms around a few wrestling players, this was the real thing. By the time it was over, the flying spikes and fists had taken their toll on both rosters. The game only continued after umpire Cece Carlucci ordered both benches to the showers and directed the park's security forces to line the perimeter of the field.

A more likely inspiration for the Stars' contentious ways than the knocks on their naked knees was Bobby Bragan, the club's player-manager from 1953 through 1955. Succeeding the Pittsburgh Pirates–bound Haney at the Hollywood helm after the 1952 championship season, Bragan brought with him from his National League career with Philadelphia and Brooklyn in the 1940s a reputation for umpire baiting and outrageous behavior. Whether his antics were contrived or spontaneous, they rarely failed to entertain the spectators or rile the men in blue.

Falling behind the hated Angels in one game, for example, Bragan infuriated them and the umpires by sending nine consecutive pinch hitters to the plate during one at bat (he kept shuffling them in after they had been announced but before the pitcher had a chance to throw a single pitch). On another occasion, after being ejected from a game, he sent his sixteen-year-old batboy to take his place in the third base coach's box. Perhaps his most memorable stunt took place during a losing effort against San Diego in 1953. Handling the catching chores this day, he vented his frustration with the way the ball and strike calls had been going by ripping off his chest protector and furiously slamming it to the ground. Directed by the umpire to retrieve it, Bragan ignored the order, proceeding instead to remove his shin guards, mask, glove, and cap, and throwing them, one at a time, onto the field. Tossed from the game for this display, Bragan continued his impromptu striptease from the dugout, adding his uniform top, shoes, socks, and a few towels to the pile of equipment and laundry before him.

Bragan and the Stars survived the fine and suspension the league levied on him for this performance and handily won the pennant in 1953, but Bragan's short fuse did not always provide humor or good example. In August 1954, with his club in a tight battle with San Diego for

PLAYERS BRAWL AS STARS, ANGELS DIVIDE

KAYO KELLEHER—Fistic fireworks explode in sixth inning of first Star-Angel game as Hollywood's Frankie Kelleher, protesting a duster pitch, ignites free-for-all. Left photo: Kelleher, No. 7, throws left at Angels' Fred Richards as Twinks' Gordy Maltzberger, right, tries to separate bout. Right photo: Kelleher (head and arm showing) has already knocked Richards down and out of picture and is being restrained by teammate Eddie Malone, No. 10. At right, Stars' Ted Beard, No. 26, and Jack Phillips, hold enraged Angel Pitcher Joe Hatten. Moments before, Kelleher had knocked down Hatten and that's when Richards came in to help.

SPORTS PARADE

BY BRAVEN DYER

[Ray Canton, former local baseball writer now slaving for the Chicago Tribune, buzzed Bob Lemon, ace Cleveland hurler, the other day, and sent along this guest column.]

Baseball's two greatest pitchers are from old Philadelphia, says Bob Lemon, 32-year-old pitching ace of the Cleveland Indians. He means, of course, Robin Roberts of the National League Phillies and Bobby Shantz of the American League Athletics.

The 6-foot, 185-pound Lemon, who grew up in Long Beach, brushed aside a reference to his own record over the past five seasons as he sat in a big chair in a room he shared with Catcher Jim Hegan in Chicago's Congress Hotel a couple of hours before Cleveland played the White Sox the other day. Lemon's record from 1948 through 1952 includes more victories in that period than any other hurler in the major leagues. He no-hitter against Detroit on June 30, 1948. In addition, he hurled two triumphs in the 1948 World Series against the Boston Braves.

"I saw Roberts pitch last summer in the All-Star game in Chicago. I have looked up his record and checked it. And I am sure he is the greatest right-hander in the game.

"He has control, stamina and real good stuff. He's big and strong and can work a lot. I like the way he paces himself. Correct pacing is tough to learn. He can give you that little extra when he's in a tight spot. Yes, I've heard it said that he isn't too fast. I've talked to some of the National League hitters about that. They tell me that when Roberts goes into the ninth with a one-run lead, he can really show you something with his fast ball.

PRAISES SHANTZ

"I'm never sure that Shantz has a sore arm. He's no flash in the pan. He's the greatest left-hander in the game. He'll be around for a long while. Since Bobby's in our league I graded Shantz when I first saw Hal Newhouser of Detroit when he was the talk of our league in 1946 and 1947. Shantz is just as good. Pound for pound that little

Turn to Page 4, Column 1

HOT CORNER HEAT—The sixth inning of opener continues to sizzle as second brawl breaks out minutes after Kelleher incident. Angel Pitcher Cal McLish, dashing into battle from dugout, pulls Beard from melee with Seraphs' Third-sacker Murray Franklin, who is somewhere in pile. Beard spiked Franklin in slide.

Times photos by Larry Sharkey

Players Riot as Twinks, Angels Split

Continued from Page 1, Part 1

and others collected assorted scratches and bruises. The Stars' Mel Queen appeared to inflict the most punishment—and may get a shot at Rocky Marciano of the American League.

Franklin and Beard were ejected when the umpires once got things in hand.

Fortunately, there was no "audience participation." With an overflow throng of 10,468 present, a serious riot might have ensued had fans begun joining the melee.

Record Attendance

That turnout swelled the series total to 63,017, thus shattering the former high of 62,311 established in 1947. The Stars' home gate now is some 10,000 ahead of last year.

Oh, yes, the ball games.

Well, George O'Connell captured his 15th victory in the opener by scattering four hits. He had a perfecto in the making until two were out in the sixth, when Richards singled infield. And his shutout vanished in the next frame when Gene Baker scored from third as Les Peden grounded out.

Kelleher's batting was enough to win for the Stars, but they added two more tallies in the seventh as Hatten was belted out.

Randy Gumpert pitched and batted the Angels to victory after intermission. He personally singled across Los Angeles' first two scores and stopped a last-inning rally with the tying tally at the plate.

Red Munger was the loser.

The split gave Hollywood a 5-3 series decision and maintained

Turn to Page 3, Column 2

Cardinals Erupt, Crush Brooks, 10-1

ST. LOUIS, Aug. 2 (AP)—The St. Louis Cardinals, defeated six straight times by Brooklyn, drubbed the league-leading Dodgers today, 10-1, as two ailing Redbirds—Red Schoendienst and Steve Bilko—swung powerful bats to back the sharp six-hit pitching of Harvey Haddix.

Lefty Haddix, gaining his 13th victory against only four defeats, issued two walks. The only run he yielded brought on a rhubarb that led to the banishment of Catcher Sal Yvars.

Podres Chased

Johnny Podres, rookie Brooklyn southpaw, was knocked out for the first time in his last four starts and suffered his first defeat in eight decisions since April 23 as St. Louis pounded out 12 hits, which included three doubles and three home runs.

Bilko, felled last night by a hard bad-hopping grounder that struck him in the left ear and sent him to a hospital for X rays, delivered a single and a grand-slam homer, his 14th home run of the year. X rays showed no bone fractures.

Ray Jablonski also homered for the Cardinals, belting his 16th of the season with a teammate aboard in the first inning.

BASEBALL STANDINGS

PACIFIC COAST LEAGUE

	W	L	Pct.
HOLLYWOOD	81	51	.614
Seattle	74	61	.548
LOS ANGELES	69	64	.519
San Francisco	66	68	.493
Portland	65	67	.492
San Diego	60	72	.454
Oakland	60	73	.451
Sacramento	59	78	.431

*Games behind leader.

Yesterday's Results

HOLLYWOOD, 4-2; LOS ANGELES, 2-3.
Oakland, 4; San Francisco, 3-2 (1st game, 15 innings).
Seattle, 5-0; Portland, 1-1.
Sacramento, 3-2; San Diego, 0-5.

New Series Ended

HOLLYWOOD, 5; LOS ANGELES, 3.
Seattle, 5; Portland, 4.
San Francisco, 7; Oakland, 3.
San Diego, 5; Sacramento, 3.

Games Tonight

Sacramento (Gumbert) at Hollywood (Karcher) 8:15.
San Francisco (Gaven) at Los Angeles (Fannin) 8:15.
Seattle (Kinnaman, 12-8) at Oakland (Bamberger, 12-8).
San Diego (Kerrigan, 11-13) at Portland.
Only games scheduled.

AMERICAN LEAGUE

	W	L	Pct.	*GB
New York	68	35	.660	
Chicago	62	46	.574	8½
Cleveland	59	46	.562	10
Boston	54	49	.524	14
Washington	53	51	.510	15½
Philadelphia	46	58	.442	22½
Detroit	38	65	.369	30
St. Louis	38	68	.358	31½

*Games behind leader

Yesterday's Results

Washington, 1; Chicago, 0.
Cleveland, 10-7; Philadelphia, 1-1.
Detroit, 2-0; Boston, 1-6.
St. Louis at New York, postponed.

Games Today

St. Louis (Cain, 4-5) at New York (Ford, 11-4).
Chicago (Pierce, 12-7) at Washington (Schmitz, 2-5), night.
Only games scheduled.

NATIONAL LEAGUE

	W	L	Pct.	*GB
Brooklyn	66	35	.653	
Milwaukee	59	43	.578	7½
Philadelphia	53	43	.552	10½
St. Louis	50	49	.505	15
New York	48	49	.495	16
Cincinnati	45	58	.437	22
Chicago	40	62	.392	26½
Pittsburgh	32	74	.302	35½

*Games behind leader

Yesterday's Results

St. Louis, 10; Brooklyn, 1.
Philadelphia, 4-2; Milwaukee, 1-6.
New York, 5; Pittsburgh, 3.
Cincinnati at Chicago, postponed, darkness.

Major Leaders

BY THE ASSOCIATED PRESS

AMERICAN LEAGUE

		AB	R	H	Pct.
Vernon, Wash.					.337
Kell, Boston					
Rosen, Cleveland					

NATIONAL LEAGUE

		AB	R	H	Pct.
Schoendienst, St.L.					
Irvin, New York					

HOME RUNS

American League—...
National League—...

RUNS BATTED IN

American League—...
National League—...

TODAY IN SPORTS

HORSE RACING—Del Mar, 2 p.m.

BASEBALL—Sacramento vs. Hollywood, Gilmore Field, 8:15 p.m.

WRESTLING—Hollywood Legion Stadium, 8:30 p.m.

Frank Kelleher, a Hollywood Stars veteran, stormed the mound after being intentionally nailed by Angels pitcher Joe Hatten, sparking the famous August 2, 1953, riot between the two teams at Gilmore Field. (National Baseball Library and Archive, Cooperstown, N.Y.)

Colorful and outrageous Hollywood Stars player-manager Bobby Bragan shakes the hand of his first baseman, Dale Long, ca. 1954. (Dick Dobbins Collection.)

Trans-formation in the Fifties

another pennant, Carlos Bernier displayed a little fire of his own, taking a swing at the home plate umpire over a strike call. Suspended for the rest of the season, Bernier not only lost a chance to lead the league in stolen bases but almost certainly cost his team the title. Deprived of his .313 bat and his speed for the final fifty games of the campaign, the Stars ended in a tie with the Padres and then lost the play-off.

If the Stars had the most volatile manager in the league, the Angels had the most explosive player in Steve Bilko. Beginning his professional career in 1945 with Allentown of the Inter-State League, Bilko arrived in Los Angeles a decade later after visiting five other junior circuits and spreading 266 major league games, mostly with the St. Louis Cardinals, over a six-year period from 1949 to 1954. Big-muscled and thick-waisted, the six-foot-one, 240-pound slugger presented a terrifying figure at the plate. His numbers supported the power image he cast. After leading the Piedmont League with 20 home runs and a .333 average in a partial season with Lynchburg in 1948, and then pounding International League pitching for 34 home runs and 125 RBIs the next year with Rochester, Bilko earned his first call-up with the Cardinals. But misfortune plagued his major league career. A broken arm in 1952 limited his playing time, and strength at first base in the St. Louis organization pushed him down the depth chart behind "Nippy" Jones and Dick Sisler. Although he put in a full season for the Redbirds in 1953, he struck out a league-leading 125 times, 5 of them coming in one particularly inglorious game on May 28. Despite his 21 homers and 84 RBIs, the Cardinals thought they would be better served by moving one of their outfielders—Bilko's fellow Pennsylvanian Stan Musial—to first base. St. Louis sold Bilko to the Cubs in April 1954, but he found little playing time as Dee Fondy's backup, and at the end of the season Chicago released him to Los Angeles.

The Angels provided a new lease on Bilko's checkered career and he responded spectacularly. For the next three years Bilko feasted on PCL pitching in a way that had not been seen since the days of Smead Jolley and Buzz Arlett. In 1955 he batted .328, drove in 124 runs, and clouted 37 homers. That performance gained him league MVP honors. For the pennant-winning Angels in 1956 he boosted his average to .360 and his RBI and home run output to 164 and 55, respectively. Those league-leading totals in each category helped Bilko become the first Triple Crown winner in the PCL since 1940, when the Angels' Lou Novikoff, "The Mad Russian," overpowered the league with 41 homers, 171 RBIs, 259 hits, and a .363 average. Needless to say, Steve Bilko easily won another MVP award, joining Oakland's Les Scarsella as the league's only other two-time recipient of this high honor. Scarsella had earned his MVP trophies in 1944 with a league-best .329 batting average and again in 1946 on .322 hitting, 22 homers, and 91 RBIs in just 121 games; Bilko's, of course, came in consecutive years, a unique feat in league history. The loss to the majors of several of Bilko's teammates on the 1956 championship team—Gene Mauch (.348, 20 homers, 84 RBIs), Bob Speake (.300, 20, 111), and Dave Hillman (21-7), for example—relegated the Seraphs to the second division in 1957, but Bilko never missed a beat in his assault on the PCL record books. His 140 RBIs and 56 round-trippers again led the league. And for an unprecedented third year in a row, the league named him its MVP.

Bilko's gaudy numbers—148 home runs, 428 RBIs, 379 runs scored—in those three PCL seasons earned him another crack at the majors with Cincinnati in 1958. But by late June he was back on the West Coast, playing ball in Wrigley Field, though not with the Angels and not in the Pacific Coast League. Traded with Johnny Klippstein for Don Newcombe, Bilko now wore Dodger—L.A. Dodger, National League Dodger—blue. The majors had finally reached the Pacific.

The shifts of the Giants to San Francisco and the Dodgers to Los Angeles after the 1957 major league season were presaged in the successive transfers of clubs from Boston, St. Louis, and Philadelphia to Milwaukee (1953), Baltimore (1954), and Kansas City (1955), respectively—moves that ended fifty years of franchise stability in the majors. Surviving two

The 1956 Pacific Coast League championship trophy is shown here at Wrigley Field along with Steve Bilko (left) of the Los Angeles Angels, who holds his MVP award. Bob Anderson (center) was voted the Most Valuable Rookie. Angels manager Bob Scheffing (far right) looks on. (Dick Dobbins Collection.)

1956 P.C.L. CHAMPS

LOS ANGELES ANGELS

An autographed team photo of the 1956 PCL champion Los Angeles Angels. (Dick Dobbins Collection.)

world wars, the Great Depression, and its own occasional housekeeping problems and anachronistic policies, Major League Baseball reluctantly agreed that the times and conditions of business were changing in the postwar world of a baby boom, television, suburban sprawl, and consumer indulgence. Their teams playing in rapidly aging and antiquated facilities, often located in deteriorating inner-city neighborhoods, major league magnates fearfully watched overall attendance at their parks drop over 30 percent from nearly 21 million in 1948 to 14.5 million in 1953.

The National League franchises in Brooklyn and New York fully mirrored this situation. Walter O'Malley's Dodgers had drawn 1.8 million in 1946 and 1947, but, despite five pennants over the next ten years and no finish lower than third, attendance at Ebbets Field declined steadily until it bottomed out near one million in 1957. The situation at the Polo Grounds was worse. Willie Mays, the 1951 "miracle of Coogan's Bluff," and the four-game sweep of the Cleveland Indians in the 1954 World Series notwithstanding, the Giants saw their postwar attendance peak at 1.6 million in 1947 and then plummet to a mere 654,000 a decade later. Although located in the nation's most populous city and the bearers of an unparalleled baseball tradition, the Giants averaged only 9,000 fans at their home games in 1957, less than a third of what the Braves were drawing to County Stadium in Milwaukee. Staking a claim for the major league game in new territory proved an irresistible example. As it had attracted daring and hopeful easterners to seek their fortunes in gold country a century earlier, California now beckoned new emigrants to find riches in the green playing fields of a game that the original Forty-niners had brought with them.

The arrival of the Giants and the Dodgers deprived the Pacific Coast League of its two principal markets and effected changes not only in the league's lineup but also in its status. Actually, the PCL had assumed a new look before the National League clubs opened play on the West Coast, for after the 1955 season the Oakland franchise had skipped across the Canadian border and established a new home in Vancouver, British Columbia. The desertion of one of the league's charter franchises provided a western version of the tale of financial woe that prompted New York and Brooklyn to make their moves. Faced with a rotting ballpark, whose outfield fence occasionally relinquished planks on hard-hit drives against it, and miserable attendance (lowest in the league in 1955 with 141,397), Oaks owner Brick Laws found Vancouver's long baseball tradition and five-year-old Capilano Stadium very much to his liking. Although the renamed Mounties finished last in the PCL in 1956, a showing that influenced Laws to sell the club to a local businessmen's group after its initial season, they climbed to second a year later, drawing the league's highest attendance in the process. With solid pitching from George Bamberger, Ervin Palica, and Chuck Estrada, Vancouver remained a competitive first-division team for the rest of the 1950s.

As the Pacific Coast League went international and the National League bicoastal, the transformation of the venerable PCL quickened its pace. Having purchased the Angels franchise in February 1957, O'Malley had a ballpark waiting for him in Los Angeles should the Dodgers move. Giants owner Horace Stoneham, who always contended that he had decided to take his club out of New York prior to and independent of the Dodgers' decision, secured an agreement with the city of San Francisco that called for the construction of a municipal ballpark and provided for the use of Seals Stadium in the meantime.[3] The imminent displacement of the Angels also affected the Hollywood Stars. Deprived of their competitive partner in the L.A. baseball market and reduced to a sideshow

An inscribed home plate used in 1955 during the last home game played by the Oaks at the Emeryville ballpark. Shortly after the game, the ballpark was demolished. The team moved to Vancouver in 1956. (Photograph by Doug McWilliams. Dick Dobbins Collection.)

with the arrival of the Dodgers, the Stars prepared to move as well. At their winter meetings after the 1957 season, league owners and officials approved the franchise transfers of the Angels to Spokane, the Seals to Phoenix, and the Stars, ironically, to Salt Lake City, whence the club had come in 1926. The movement of these key PCL franchises to less populous cities and smaller ballparks meant that the league no longer met the conditions for the open classification status it had enjoyed since 1952. The Coast League dropped to Class AAA for the start of the 1958 season, where it has been ever since. However faint or unrealistic its major league aspirations had been, the termination of its unique standing in organized baseball buried them completely.

Because Seals Stadium accommodated the Giants before Candlestick Park opened in 1960, and Wrigley Field hosted the expansion Angels of the American League in 1961, these wonderful, weathered PCL parks still had some life in them. The same could not be said for Gilmore Field and Oaks Park, however, which, like the Polo Grounds and Ebbets Field, fell to the wrecking balls within a short time after their abandonment. Even at Seals and Wrigley, though, the extended seasons were clearly an epilogue, a remembrance of the glory days, not a rehearsal for more to come. Occasionally, the echoes of the past could be heard, perhaps the most resounding provided by Steve Bilko, the last superstar of the old Pacific Coast League. Given another shot at the majors with the new Angels, the thirty-three-year-old veteran finally had a year in the show that

Fans leaving the Seals' stadium in San Francisco for the last time in 1959. Demolition of the ballpark began a few days later. (Photograph by Leo Cohen. The Oakland Tribune Collection.)

matched the promise of his MVP years in the PCL during the mid-1950s. Alternating at first base with Ted Kluszewski, the former Cincinnati slugger, Bilko blasted twenty homers over Wrigley's familiar fences, batted a respectable .279, and turned in the best defensive work of anyone on the team. True to form, he also struck out almost 30 percent of the time, though his .544 slugging average attested to the damage he could do when he connected.

A brilliant PCL player but a flawed major leaguer, Bilko personified the league that provided the best showcase for his abilities and idiosyncracies. Both were legendary. His Ruthian work at the plate during his MVP years was matched with an appetite for food and drink that would have made the Babe proud. Trying to keep his weight down after a hard night on the town, Steve often resorted to locking himself in the bathroom, stuffing towels in the door and window cracks, and turning on the hot water full blast to create a private steam bath. The pounds he lost through this method and the day's game were promptly restored during the next evening's carousing. A strange regimen, perhaps, but no less effective or curious than Lou Novikoff's ritual of having his wife sit in a box seat behind home plate with instructions to taunt him as loudly as she could. Esther's verbal abuse inspired Lou to respond with his bat and helped generate a Triple Crown performance in 1940 and a .300 batting average for the Chicago Cubs in 1942.

Rapid Fire

PCL games were played rapidly, averaging two hours and twelve minutes during the 1955 season. Moderate use of relief pitching and hitters who tended to business in the batter's box were two major factors. In addition, league president Leslie M. O'Connor had instructed the umpires to keep the games moving at all times.

The characters and the color did not disappear with the transformation of the Pacific Coast League in 1958. Its reputation for producing sluggers at the plate, aces on the mound, and zaniness in the park has been upheld over the course of numerous franchise shifts and realignments, including the introduction of a divisional organization in 1963. The purveyors of PCL power who have made a successful transition to the majors form an impressive list: Willie McCovey topped the Coast League with 29 home runs in only 92 games for Phoenix in 1959 before completing the year with the Giants and earning National League Rookie of the Year honors; Willie Kirkland led the PCL in both homers (34) and RBIs (97) for the Honolulu Islanders in 1957 before joining the Giants a season later; Dave Kingman launched a few trademark shots for Phoenix in 1971 that quickly earned him the label "King Kong"; Steve Ontiveros was named Minor League Player of the Year in 1973 for a stellar season with Phoenix that included a .357 average, 32 doubles, and 16 triples; and Albuquerque's Mike Marshall brought another Player of the Year award to the PCL in 1981 with the league's first Triple Crown season (.373, 34 homers, 137 RBIs) since Steve Bilko's in 1956. Add to this list the names of Tommy Davis and Willie Davis (Spokane), Brooks Robinson (Vancouver), Deron Johnson (San Diego), Jesus Alou (Tacoma), Tony Oliva (Dallas–Ft. Worth), Tony Perez (San Diego), Graig Nettles (Denver), Bobby Bonds (Phoenix), Davey Lopes, Ron Cey, and Pedro Guerrero (Albuquerque), Danny Tartabull (Calgary), and John Kruk (Las Vegas) and it's easy to see why the transit lines between the Pacific Coast League and the majors are kept busy.

Runs,

Hits,

and

an Era

Although the PCL has been generally regarded as a hitter's league, its steady stream of pitchers to the majors has been no less outstanding.

Inspired by the verbal abuse of his wife, Esther, Lou "The Mad Russian" Novikoff won the Triple Crown in 1940 and sparked the Los Angeles Angels to a second-place finish for the season. (Dick Dobbins Collection.)

Willie McCovey left the PCL's Phoenix team midseason in 1959 to join the San Francisco Giants. In only a half season of major league play, McCovey earned the coveted National League Rookie of the Year award. He is pictured here with teammate Orlando Cepeda (right). (FN-29912. California Historical Society, San Francisco.)

Knuckleballers Phil Niekro (Denver) and Wilbur Wood (Seattle) baffled PCL batters in the early 1960s before tossing years of frustration at major league hitters. Luis Tiant had a season in 1964 much like McCovey's five years earlier. Posting fifteen wins against only one defeat for Portland, the good-natured Cuban joined Cleveland in midseason and tossed a four-hit shutout against the Yankees in his debut. He finished his rookie season with a 10-4 mark and a 2.83 ERA. Another Latin player, Panamanian Juan Berenguer, fanned 220 PCL batters for Tacoma in 1979, the most since Sam Jones did it to 246 batters in 1951. Others who practiced their craft on the West Coast before enjoying solid careers in the majors included Ferguson Jenkins (Little Rock), Rick Rhoden (Albuquerque), Mike Bielecki (Honolulu), Gaylord Perry (Tacoma), and Dave Stewart

(Albuquerque). Even Bo Belinski (Honolulu), trying to rediscover in 1968–69 the magic in his arm that made him L.A.'s darling in the early 1960s, and ageless Satchell Paige (Portland), offering his "two-hump blooper" and "hesitation pitch" for a few memorable innings in 1961, helped define the special character of the Pacific Coast League. No less so was Vancouver's Tom Drees, an undistinguished twenty-six-year-old coming off arthroscopic surgery who stepped into the record books in 1989 with three no-hitters in a single season. The majors, however, looked at his 9-11 mark and 4-plus ERA in his other games and declined an invitation to their show.

Apart from the performances that merited trips to the majors or provided a particular season's highlight, there were moments that reminded old-timers of the PCL's tradition for outrageous and daft behavior. Portland's "Sweet Lou" Piniella, his nickname an ironic commentary on his fiery temper, once attempted to vent his frustration for striking out with the bases loaded by kicking the outfield fence. Unfortunately for Lou, the fence fought back. Piniella's assault loosened a fifteen-foot section that collapsed on him before he could get away, and it took the grounds crew several long, embarrassing minutes to unpin him. Perhaps because it was the only original PCL city to continue to have a team after 1968, Portland seemed to have more than its fair share of wacky events. In 1984, Pam Postema, the first female umpire to make it to Triple A, tossed Beavers manager Lee Elia, most of his players, and even the batboy from a game. The latter drew Postema's ire when he ignored her order to retrieve a chair that Elia had thrown out on the field.

If these incidents had the ring of the old Pacific Coast League to them, they were faint echoes of the real thing. From 1903 to 1958 only thirteen cities hosted PCL franchises. A few, like Tacoma, Fresno, Venice, and Vancouver, fielded teams for only a season or two during this period. The others underscored the league's remarkable stability and the intense loyalties and rivalries that stemmed from it. In many respects those rivalries transcended the ball games, providing a context for forging civic pride and bolstering competitive self-images. Although proximate geography largely fueled the natural rivalries between Portland and Seattle, San Francisco and Oakland, and Los Angeles and Hollywood, something more was at stake when the Bay City Seals took on the Los Angeles Angels. The diamond provided a surrogate arena in "a Darwinian competition" between the two to be the West Coast's premier city.[4]

Prompted by civic leaders to overcome their intraurban differences in a common effort to be the best, residents of San Francisco and Los Angeles rallied to their respective banners of Golden Gate orange and blue or red and blue in a concerted attempt to assert their hegemony. In the search for real and symbolic affirmations of their distinctive identities, both cities eagerly embraced baseball and the "victories" over the alien culture of the other that it provided. The major league rivalry between the Giants and the Dodgers not only carried the passionate tenor of the Brooklyn–New York encounter across a continent but also reflected the unique strains of the California experience in the tournament between the state's two principal cities. After 1958, another twenty cities—from Honolulu to Little Rock, Calgary to Tucson—would land a franchise in the Pacific Coast League. Their far-flung locations and often temporary participation did not preclude first-rate ball on their fields. They did, however, forfeit a chance for the kind of continuity and character that clearly marked the old PCL.

When the Coast League realigned in 1958 to accommodate the arrival of the Giants and the Dodgers, league officials decided to start a new and separate set of season statistics. Practically, that decision reflected the adoption of a 154-game schedule, one identical with the majors at that time, and the appropriateness of distinguishing player and team performances between seasons of very different lengths. Symbolically, however, the decision had the effect of storing in a vault the era in which the original PCL records had been made.

A youth center now sits on the site of Wrigley Field, a nursery where Gilmore once stood, an auto mart on the acre where the DiMaggio brothers and Lefty O'Doul won pennants for the Seals. Only photographs and ever-dimming memories recall the games that were played there and the pure joy they evoked. Yet, as surely as the records of those times enjoy a special status, so too the league they chronicled merits a fond and bittersweet remembrance. For much more than a minor pastime or a distant reflection of the show back East, the Pacific Coast League in its fifty-five-year prime celebrated a game and enriched an entire section of the country through its pursuit.

Notes

1. Salsinger, "Here's P.C.L.'s Side," 43.
2. Beverage, *The Hollywood Stars*, 183.
3. Sullivan, *The Dodgers Move West*, 117, 133.
4. Issel and Cherney, *San Francisco*, 202–3; Lotchin, "The Darwinian City," 365.

Appendix 1

PCL All-Star Teams

1928 All-Star Team (voted on by twenty-one sports-writers in PCL cities)

1B	Earl Sheely (Sacramento)
2B	Johnny Kerr (Hollywood)
3B	James McLaughlin (Sacramento)
SS	Lyn Lary, (Oakland)
LF	Roy Johnson (San Francisco)
CF	Earl Averill (San Francisco)
RF	Smead Jolley (San Francisco)
Sub	Hollis Thurston (San Francisco)
C	John Bassler (Hollywood)
P	Dutch Ruether (San Francisco)

1934 All-Star Team (selected by newspaper ballot of fans; lost postseason series, four games to two, to 1934 Los Angeles Angels)

1B	Babe Dahlgren (Mission)
2B	Al Wright (Mission)
3B	Joe Coscarart (Seattle)
3B	Fred Haney (Hollywood)
SS	Jim Levey (Hollywood)
OF	Ox Eckhardt (Mission)
OF	Smead Jolley (Hollywood)
OF	Mike Hunt (Seattle)
OF	Louis Almada (Mission)
C	John Bassler (Hollywood)
C	Larry Woodall (San Francisco)
P	Joe Sullivan (Hollywood)
P	Herman Pillette (Seattle)
P	LeRoy Herrmann (San Francisco)
P	Sam Gibson (San Francisco)
P	Clarence Mitchell (Mission)
Mgr	Dutch Ruether (Seattle)

Paul Zingg's All-Time PCL All-Star Team (players with minimum of three PCL seasons, 1903–58)

1B	Steve Bilko (Los Angeles)
2B	Hugh Luby (Oakland, San Francisco)
3B	Frank Brazill (Portland, Seattle, Los Angeles, Mission)
SS	Raymond French (Vernon, Sacramento, Oakland)
OF	Buzz Arlett (Oakland)
OF	Jigger Statz (Los Angeles)
OF	Smead Jolley (San Francisco, Hollywood, Oakland)
C	Billy Raimondi (Oakland, Sacramento, Los Angeles)
RHP	Frank Shellenback (Vernon, Sacramento, Hollywood, San Diego)
LHP	Tony Freitas (Sacramento, Portland)
Sub	Lou Novikoff, OF (Los Angeles, Seattle)
Sub	Ox Eckhardt, OF (Mission)
Sub	Paul Strand, OF (Salt Lake City, Portland)
Sub	Sam Gibson, RHP (San Francisco, Portland, Oakland)
Sub	Harry Krause, LHP (Portland, Oakland, Mission)
Sub	Artie Wilson, SS (San Diego, Oakland, Seattle, Portland, Sacramento)
Sub	Truck Hannah, C (Sacramento, Salt Lake City, Vernon, Los Angeles)
Sub	Dick Gyselmen, 3B (Mission, Seattle, San Diego)
Mgr	Lefty O'Doul (San Francisco, San Diego, Oakland, Vancouver, Seattle)

Appendix 2

PCL Records

All-Time PCL Career Leaders

Games played	Jigger Statz	2,790
Years in league	Herman Pillette	23
At bats	Jigger Statz	10,657
Total bases	Jigger Statz	4,405
Runs scored	Jigger Statz	1,996
Hits	Jigger Statz	3,356
Singles	Jigger Statz	2,564
Doubles	Jigger Statz	595
Triples	Jigger Statz	137
Home runs	Buzz Arlett	251
RBIs	Buzz Arlett	1,188
Stolen bases	Billy Lane	468
Batting average	Ox Eckhardt	.382
Games pitched	Herman Pillette	708
Innings pitched	Frank Shellenback	4,185
Games won	Frank Shellenback	295
Games lost	Charles Baum	235
Complete games	Frank Shellenback	361
Strikeouts	Dick Barrett	1,866

Appendix 3

PCL Annual Statistics and Team Standings, 1903-58

The first table in this appendix was excerpted from O'Neal, *The Pacific Coast League;* the remaining tables were excerpted from *The Encyclopedia of Minor League Baseball.* A slash (/) indicates a change in franchise location or a change in a player's team affiliation (e.g., Seattle/Tacoma means that the Seattle franchise moved to Tacoma during the season).

1903

	W	L	GB
Los Angeles	133	78	—
Sacramento	105	105	27½
Seattle	98	100	28½
San Francisco	107	110	29
Portland	95	108	34
Oakland	89	126	46

Ave. Harry Lumley, Seattle, .387
HRs   Truck Egan, Sacramento, 13
Wins Doc Newton, Los Angeles, 35

1904

	W	L	GB
Tacoma*	130	94	—
Los Angeles**	119	97	7
Seattle	114	106	14
Oakland	116	109	14½
San Francisco	101	117	26
Portland	79	136	46½

*Won first half of a split season.
**Won second half of a split season.
Play-off: Tacoma 5 games, Los Angeles 4 games

Ave. Emil Frisk, Seattle, .337
HRs   Truck Eagan, Tacoma, 25
Wins Doc Newton, Los Angeles, 39

1905

	W	L	GB
Los Angeles*	120	94	—
San Francisco	125	100	½
Tacoma**/Sacramento	106	107	13
Oakland	103	117	20
Portland	94	110	21
Seattle	93	111	22

*Won second half of a split season.
**Won first half of a split season before moving.
Play-off: Los Angeles 5 games, Tacoma/Sacramento 1 game, 1 tie

Ave. Kitty Brashear, Los Angeles, .303
HRs   Truck Eagan, Tacoma, 21
Wins James Whalen, San Francisco, 30

1906

	W	L	GB
Portland	114	59	—
Seattle	97	83	20½
San Francisco	93	81	21½
Los Angeles	93	91	26½
Oakland	78	106	41½
Fresno	64	119	55

Ave. Michael Mitchell, Portland, .351
HRs   Michael Mitchell, Portland, 6
Wins Rube Vickers, Seattle, 39

1907

	W	L	GB
Los Angeles	115	74	—
San Francisco	104	99	17
Oakland	97	101	21½
Portland	72	114	41½

Ave. Truck Eagan, Oakland, .335
HRs   Walter Carlisle, Los Angeles, 14
Wins Dolly Gray, Los Angeles, 32

1908

	W	L	GB
Los Angeles	110	78	—
Portland	95	90	13½
San Francisco	100	104	18
Oakland	83	116	32½

Ave.   Babe Danzig, Portland, .298
HRs   Henry Heitmuller, Oakland, 12
Wins   Bob Groom, Portland, 29

1909

	W	L	GB
San Francisco	132	80	—
Portland	112	87	13½
Los Angeles	118	97	15½
Sacramento	97	107	31
Oakland	88	125	44½
Vernon	80	131	51½

Ave.   Henry Melchior, San Francisco, .298
HRs   Otis Johnson, Portland, 13
Wins   Frank Browning, San Francisco, 32

1910

	W	L	GB
Portland	114	87	—
Oakland	122	98	1½
San Francisco	114	106	9½
Vernon	113	107	10½
Los Angeles	101	121	23½
Sacramento	83	128	36

Ave.   Hunky Shaw, San Francisco, .281
HRs   Ping Bodie, San Francisco, 30
Wins   Cack Henley, San Francisco, 34

1911

	W	L	GB
Portland	113	79	—
Vernon	118	88	2
Oakland	111	99	11
Sacramento	95	109	24
San Francisco	95	112	25½
Los Angeles	82	127	39½

Ave.   Buddy Ryan, Portland, .333
HRs   Buddy Ryan, Portland, 23
Wins   Bill Steen, Portland, 30

1912

	W	L	GB
Oakland	120	83	—
Vernon	118	83	1
Los Angeles	110	93	10
Portland	85	100	26
San Francisco	89	115	31½
Sacramento	73	121	42½

Ave.   Henry Heitmuller, Los Angeles, .335
HRs   Bert Coy, Oakland, 19
Wins   Harry Ables, Oakland, 25
       Charles Chech, Los Angeles, 25

1913

	W	L	GB
Portland	109	86	—
Sacramento	103	94	7
Venice	107	102	9
San Francisco	104	103	11
Los Angeles	100	108	15½
Oakland	90	120	26½

Ave.   Harry Bayless, Vernon, .324
HRs   Bert Coy, Oakland, 18
Wins   Charles Fanning, San Francisco, 28

1914

	W	L	GB
Portland	113	84	—
Los Angeles	116	94	3½
San Francisco	115	96	5
Venice	113	98	7
Mission	90	121	30
Oakland	79	133	41½

Ave.   Harry Wolter, Los Angeles, .328
HRs   Ty Lober, Portland, 9
Wins   Irv Higginbotham, Portland, 31
ERA   Slim Love, Los Angeles, 1.56

1915

	W	L	GB
San Francisco	118	89	—
Salt Lake City	108	89	5
Los Angeles	110	98	8½
Vernon	102	104	15½
Oakland	93	113	24½
Portland	78	116	38½

Ave.   Harry Wolter, Los Angeles, .359
HRs   Biff Schaller, San Francisco, 20
Wins   Lefty Williams, Salt Lake City, 33
ERA   Slim Love, Los Angeles, 1.95

1916

	W	L	GB
Los Angeles	119	79	—
Vernon	115	91	8
Salt Lake City	99	96	18 1/2
San Francisco	104	102	19
Portland	93	98	26 1/2
Oakland	72	136	56

Ave.	Duke Kenworth, Oakland, .314
HRs	Bunny Brief, Salt Lake City, 33
Wins	Allen Southoron, Portland, 30
ERA	Art Fromme, Vernon, 1.92

1917

	W	L	GB
San Francisco	119	93	—
Los Angeles	116	94	2
Salt Lake City	102	97	10 1/2
Portland	98	102	15
Oakland	103	108	15 1/2
Vernon	84	128	35

Ave.	Morrie Rath, Salt Lake City, .341
HRs	Ken Williams, Portland, 24
Wins	Eric Erickson, San Francisco, 31
ERA	Eric Erickson, San Francisco, 1.93

1918

	W	L	GB
Vernon	58	44	—
Los Angeles	57	47	2
San Francisco	51	51	7
Sacramento	48	48	7
Salt Lake City	48	49	7 1/2
Oakland	40	63	18 1/2

League suspended operations July 14.
Play-off: Los Angeles 5 games, Vernon 2 games

Ave.	Art Griggs, Sacramento, .378
HRs	Art Griggs, Sacramento, 12
	Earl Sheely, Salt Lake City, 12
Wins	Doc Crandall, Los Angeles, 16
	Walt Leverenz, Salt Lake City, 16
ERA	John P. Quinn, Vernon, 1.48

1919

	W	L	GB
Vernon	111	70	—
Los Angeles	108	72	2 1/2
Salt Lake City	88	83	18
Sacramento	85	83	19 1/2
Oakland	86	96	25 1/2
San Francisco	84	94	25 1/2
Portland	78	96	29 1/2
Seattle	62	108	43 1/2

Ave.	Bill Rumler, Salt Lake City, .362
HRs	Earl Sheely, Salt Lake City, 28
Wins	Doc Crandall, Los Angeles, 28
ERA	Curly Brown, Los Angeles, 2.03

1920

	W	L	GB
Vernon	110	88	—
Seattle	102	91	5 1/2
San Francisco	103	96	7 1/2
Los Angeles	102	95	7 1/2
Salt Lake City	95	92	9 1/2
Oakland	95	103	14
Sacramento	89	109	21
Portland	81	103	21

Ave.	Earl Sheely, Salt Lake City, .371
HRs	Earl Sheely, Salt Lake City, 33
Wins	Buzz Arlett, Oakland, 29
ERA	Jim Scott, San Francisco, 2.29

1921

	W	L	GB
Los Angeles	108	80	—
Sacramento	105	80	1 1/2
San Francisco	106	82	2
Seattle	103	82	3 1/2
Oakland	101	85	6
Vernon	96	90	11
Salt Lake City	73	110	32 1/2
Portland	51	134	55 1/2

Ave.	Hack Miller, Oakland, .347
HRs	Paddy Siglin, Salt Lake City, 22
Wins	Wheezer Dell, Vernon, 28
ERA	Vic Aldridge, Los Angeles, 2.16

1922

	W	L	GB
San Francisco	127	72	—
Vernon	123	76	4
Los Angeles	111	88	16
Salt Lake City	95	106	33
Seattle	90	107	36
Oakland	88	112	39½
Portland	87	112	40
Sacramento	76	124	51½

Ave. Paul Strand, Salt Lake City, .384
RBIs Bert Ellison, San Francisco, 141
HRs Paul Strand, Salt Lake City, 28
Wins Jakie May, Vernon, 35
ERA Jakie May, Vernon, 1.84

1923

	W	L	GB
San Francisco	124	77	—
Sacramento	112	87	11
Portland	107	89	14½
Seattle	99	97	22½
Salt Lake City	94	105	29
Los Angeles	93	109	31½
Oakland	91	111	33½
Vernon	77	122	46

Ave. Paul Strand, Salt Lake City, .394
RBIs Paul Strand, Salt Lake City, 187
HRs Paul Strand, Salt Lake City, 43
Wins Ray Kremer, Oakland, 25
ERA Vean Gregg, Seattle, 2.75

1924

	W	L	GB
Seattle	109	91	—
Los Angeles	107	92	1½
San Francisco	108	93	1½
Oakland	103	99	7
Salt Lake City	101	100	8½
Vernon	97	104	12½
Portland	88	110	20
Sacramento	88	112	21

Ave. Duffy Lewis, Salt Lake City, .392
RBIs Bert Ellison, San Francisco, 188
HRs Jim Poole, Portland, 38
Wins Willis Mitchell, San Francisco, 28
ERA Doc Crandall, Los Angeles, 2.71

1925

	W	L	GB
San Francisco	128	71	—
Salt Lake City	116	84	12½
Seattle	103	91	22½
Los Angeles	105	93	22½
Portland	92	104	34½
Oakland	88	112	40½
Sacramento	82	119	47
Vernon	80	120	48½

Ave. Paul Waner, San Francisco, .401
RBIs Tony Lazzeri, Salt Lake City, 222
HRs Tony Lazzeri, Salt Lake City, 60
Wins Clyde Barfoot, Vernon, 26
ERA Doug McWeeney, San Francisco, 2.70

1926

	W	L	GB
Los Angeles	121	81	—
Oakland	111	92	9½
Mission	106	94	14
Portland	100	101	20½
Sacramento	99	102	21½
Hollywood	94	107	26½
Seattle	89	111	31
San Francisco	84	116	36

Ave. Buzz Arlett, Oakland, .382
RBIs Buzz Arlett, Oakland, 140
HRs Elmer Smith, Portland, 46
Wins Bert Cole, Mission, 29
ERA Elmer Jacobs, Los Angeles, 2.20

1927

	W	L	GB
Oakland	120	75	—
San Francisco	106	90	14½
Seattle	98	92	19½
Sacramento	100	95	20
Portland	95	95	22½
Hollywood	92	104	28½
Mission	86	110	34½
Los Angeles	80	116	40½

Ave. Smead Jolley, San Francisco, .397
RBIs Smead Jolley, San Francisco, 163
HRs Elmer J. Smith, Portland, 40
Wins George Boehler, Oakland, 22
ERA John Miljus, Seattle, 2.36

1928

	W	L	GB
San Francisco*	120	71	—
Sacramento**	112	79	8
Hollywood	112	79	8
Mission	99	92	21
Oakland	91	100	29
Los Angeles	87	104	33
Portland	79	112	41
Seattle	64	127	56

*Won first half of a split season.
**Won second half of a split season.
Play-off: San Francisco 4 games, Sacramento 2 games

Ave. Smead Jolley, San Francisco, .404
RBIs Smead Jolley, San Francisco, 188
HRs   Smead Jolley, San Francisco, 45
Wins Dutch Ruether, San Francisco, 29
ERA   Elmer Jacobs, San Francisco, 2.56

1929

	W	L	GB
Mission*	123	78	—
San Francisco	114	87	9
Hollywood**	113	89	10½
Oakland	111	91	12½
Los Angeles	104	98	19½
Portland	90	112	33½
Sacramento	85	117	38½
Seattle	67	135	56½

*Won first half of a split season.
**Won second half of a split season.
Play-off: Hollywood 4 games, Mission 2 games

Ave. Ike Boone, Mission, .407
RBIs Ike Boone, Mission, 218
HRs   Ike Boone, Mission, 55
Wins Frank Shellenback, Hollywood, 26
ERA   Lefty Gomez, San Francisco, 3.43

1930

	W	L	GB
Hollywood*	119	81	—
Los Angeles**	113	84	4½
Sacramento	102	96	16
San Francisco	101	98	17½
Oakland	97	103	22
Seattle	92	107	26½
Mission	91	110	28½
Portland	81	117	37

*Won second half of a split season.
**Won first half of a split season.
Play-off: Hollywood 4 games, Los Angeles 1 game

Ave. Earl Sheely, San Francisco, .403
RBIs Earl Sheely, San Francisco, 180
HRs   David Barbee, Seattle/Hollywood, 41
Wins Ed Baecht, Los Angeles, 26
      Jimmy Zinn, San Francisco, 26
ERA   Ed Baecht, Los Angeles, 3.23

1931

	W	L	GB
San Francisco*	107	80	—
Hollywood**	104	83	3
Portland	100	87	7
Los Angeles	98	89	9
Sacramento	86	101	21
Oakland	86	101	21
Mission	84	103	23
Seattle	83	104	24

*Won second half of a split season.
**Won first half of a split season.
Play-off: San Francisco 4 games, Hollywood 0 games

Ave. Ox Eckhardt, Mission, .369
RBIs Ed Coleman, Portland, 183
HRs   David Barbee, Hollywood, 47
Wins Sam Gibson, San Francisco, 28
ERA   Sam Gibson, San Francisco, 2.48

1932

	W	L	GB
Portland	111	78	—
Hollywood	106	83	5
Sacramento	101	88	10
San Francisco	96	90	13½
Los Angeles	96	93	15
Seattle	90	96	19½
Oakland	80	107	30
Mission	71	117	39½

Ave.   Ox Eckhardt, Mission, .371
RBIs   George Burns, Seattle, 140
HRs   Fred Muller, Seattle, 38
Wins   Frank Shellenback, Hollywood, 26
ERA   Curt Davis, San Francisco, 2.24

1933

	W	L	GB
Los Angeles	114	73	—
Portland	105	77	6½
Hollywood	107	80	7
Sacramento	96	85	15
Oakland	93	92	20
San Francisco	81	106	33
Mission	79	108	35
Seattle	65	119	47½

Ave.   Ox Eckhardt, Mission, .414
RBIs   Joe DiMaggio, San Francisco, 169
HRs   Gene Lillard, Los Angeles, 43
Wins   Buck Newsom, Los Angeles, 30
ERA   William Ludolph, Oakland, 3.09

1934

	W	L	GB
Los Angeles*	137	50	—
Mission	101	85	35½
Hollywood	97	88	39
San Francisco	93	95	44½
Oakland	90	98	47½
Seattle	81	102	54
Sacramento	79	109	58½
Portland	66	117	69

*Won both halves of a split season.

Ave.   Frank Demaree, Los Angeles, .383
RBIs   Frank Demaree, Los Angeles, 173
HRs   Frank Demaree, Los Angeles, 45
Wins   Fay Thomas, Los Angeles, 28
ERA   Dutch Lieber, Mission, 2.50

1935

	W	L	GB
San Francisco*	103	70	—
Los Angeles**	98	76	5½
Oakland	91	83	12½
Portland	87	86	16
Mission	87	87	16½
Hollywood	83	89	19½
Seattle	80	93	23
Sacramento	75	100	29

*Won second half of a split season.
**Won first half of a split season.
Play-off: San Francisco 4 games, Los Angeles 2 games

Ave.   Ox Eckhardt, Mission, .399
RBIs   Joe DiMaggio, San Francisco, 173
HRs   Gene Lillard, Los Angeles, 56
Wins   Walter Beck, Mission, 23
ERA   Mike Meola, Los Angeles, 3.00

1936

	W	L	GB
Portland	96	79	—
San Diego	95	81	1½
Oakland	95	81	1½
Seattle	93	82	3
Mission	88	88	8½
Los Angeles	88	88	8½
San Francisco	83	93	13½
Sacramento	65	111	31½

Play-offs: Oakland 4 games, San Diego 1 game;
Portland 4 games, Seattle 0 games
Finals: Portland 4 games, Oakland 1 game

Ave.   Joe Marty, San Francisco, .359
RBIs   Art Hunt, Seattle, 135
HRs   Art Hunt, Seattle, 30
       Fred Muller, Seattle, 30
Wins   George Custer, Portland, 25
ERA   Lou Koupal, Seattle, 2.42

1937

	W	L	GB
Sacramento	102	76	—
San Francisco	98	80	4
San Diego	97	81	5
Portland	90	86	11
Los Angeles	90	88	12
Seattle	81	96	20½
Oakland	79	98	22½
Mission	73	105	29

Play-offs: San Diego 4 games, Sacramento 0 games;
Portland 4 games, San Francisco 0 games
Finals: San Diego 4 games, Portland 0 games

Ave.	George Detore, San Diego, .334
RBIs	Art Hunt, Seattle, 131
HRs	Art Hunt, Seattle, 39
Wins	Ad Liska, Portland, 24
ERA	Bill Shores, San Francisco, 2.47

1938

	W	L	GB
Los Angeles	105	73	—
Seattle	100	75	3½
Sacramento	95	82	9½
San Francisco	93	85	12
San Diego	92	85	12½
Portland	79	96	24½
Hollywood	79	99	26
Oakland	65	113	40

Play-offs: Sacramento 4 games, Los Angeles 1 game;
San Francisco 4 games, Seattle 1 game
Finals: Sacramento 4 games, San Francisco 1 game

Ave.	Smead Jolley, Hollywood/Oakland, .350
RBIs	Ted Norbert, San Francisco, 163
HRs	Ted Norbert, San Francisco, 30
Wins	Fred Hutchinson, Seattle, 25
ERA	Byron Humphries, San Diego, 2.33

1939

	W	L	GB
Seattle	101	73	—
San Francisco	97	78	4½
Los Angeles	97	79	5
Sacramento	88	88	14
San Diego	83	93	19
Hollywood	82	94	20
Oakland	78	98	24
Portland	75	98	25½

Play-offs: Los Angeles 4 games, Seattle 2 games;
Sacramento 4 games, San Francisco 1 game
Finals: Sacramento 4 games, Los Angeles 2 games

Ave.	Dom Dallessandro, San Diego, .368
RBIs	Rip Collins, Los Angeles, 128
HRs	Rip Collins, Los Angeles, 26
Wins	Hal Turpin, Seattle, 23
ERA	Sam Gibson, San Francisco, 2.24

1940

	W	L	GB
Seattle	112	66	—
Los Angeles	102	75	9½
Oakland	94	84	18
San Diego	92	85	19½
Sacramento	90	88	22
Hollywood	84	94	28
San Francisco	81	97	31
Portland	56	122	56

Play-offs: Seattle 4 games, Oakland 1 game; Los
Angeles 4 games, San Diego 3 games
Finals: Seattle 4 games, Los Angeles 1 game

Ave.	Lou Novikoff, Los Angeles, .363
RBIs	Lou Novikoff, Los Angeles, 171
HRs	Lou Novikoff, Los Angeles, 41
Wins	Dick Barrett, Seattle, 24
ERA	Jack Salveson, Oakland, 2.30

1941

	W	L	GB
Seattle	104	70	—
Sacramento	102	75	3½
San Diego	101	76	4½
Hollywood	85	91	20
San Francisco	81	95	24
Oakland	81	95	24
Los Angeles	72	98	30
Portland	71	97	30

Play-offs: Seattle 4 games, Hollywood 3 games;
Sacramento 4 games, San Diego 0 games
Finals: Seattle 4 games, Sacramento 3 games

Ave. John Moore, Los Angeles, .331
RBIs Froilan Fernandez, San Francisco, 129
HRs   Ted Norbert, Portland, 20
Wins Yank Terry, San Diego, 26
ERA   Yank Terry, San Diego, 2.31

1942

	W	L	GB
Sacramento	105	73	—
Los Angeles	104	74	1
Seattle	96	82	9
San Diego	91	87	14
San Francisco	88	90	17
Oakland	85	92	19½
Hollywood	75	103	30
Portland	67	110	37½

Play-offs: Seattle 4 games, Sacramento 1 game; Los
Angeles 4 games, San Diego 3 games
Finals: Seattle 4 games, Los Angeles 2 games

Ave. Ted Norbert, Portland, .378
RBIs Kermit Lewis, San Francisco, 115
HRs   Ted Norbert, Portland, 28
Wins Dick Barrett, Seattle, 27
ERA   Dick Barrett, Seattle, 1.72

1943

	W	L	GB
Los Angeles	110	45	—
San Francisco	89	66	21
Seattle	85	70	25
Portland	79	76	31
Hollywood	73	82	37
Oakland	73	82	37
San Diego	70	85	40
Sacramento	41	114	69

Play-offs: Seattle 4 games, Los Angeles 0 games; San
Francisco 4 games, Portland 2 games
Finals: San Francisco 4 games, Seattle 2 games

Ave. Andy Pafko, Los Angeles, .356
RBIs Andy Pafko, Los Angeles, 118
HRs   John Ostrowski, Los Angeles, 21
Wins Red Lynn, Los Angeles, 21
ERA   Alpha Brazie, Sacramento, 1.69

1944

	W	L	GB
Los Angeles	99	70	—
Portland	87	82	12
San Francisco	86	83	13
Oakland	86	83	13
Seattle	84	85	15
Hollywood	83	86	16
Sacramento	76	93	23
San Diego	75	94	24

Play-offs: Los Angeles 4 games, Portland 2 games;
San Francisco 4 games, Oakland 1 game
Finals: San Francisco 4 games, Los Angeles 3 games

Ave. Les Scarsella, Oakland, .329
RBIs Francis Kelleher, Hollywood, 121
HRs   Francis Kelleher, Hollywood, 29
Wins Marino Pieretti, Portland, 26
ERA   Clem Dreisewerd, Sacramento, 1.61

1945

	W	L	GB
Portland	112	68	—
Seattle	105	78	8½
Sacramento	95	85	17
San Francisco	96	87	17½
Oakland	90	93	23½
San Diego	82	101	31½
Los Angeles	77	107	37
Hollywood	73	110	40½

Play-offs: Seattle 4 games, Portland 3 games; San Francisco 4 games, Sacramento 3 games
Finals: San Francisco 4 games, Seattle 2 games

Ave.	Jo Jo White, Sacramento, .355
RBIs	Lou Vezelich, San Diego, 110
HRs	Ted Norbert, Seattle, 23
Wins	Robert Joyce, San Francisco, 31
ERA	Robert Joyce, San Francisco, 2.17

1946

	W	L	GB
San Francisco	115	68	—
Oakland	111	72	4
Hollywood	95	88	20
Los Angeles	94	89	21
Sacramento	94	92	22½
San Diego	78	108	38½
Portland	74	109	41
Seattle	74	109	41

Play-offs: San Francisco 4 games, Hollywood 0 games; Oakland 4 games, Los Angeles 3 games
Finals: San Francisco 4 games, Oakland 2 games

Ave.	Harvey Storey, Los Angeles/Portland, .326
RBIs	Ferris Fain, San Francisco, 112
HRs	Lloyd Christopher, Los Angeles, 26
Wins	Larry Jansen, San Francisco, 30
ERA	Larry Jansen, San Francisco, 1.57

1947

	W	L	GB
Los Angeles	106	81	—
San Francisco	105	82	1
Portland	97	89	8½
Oakland	96	90	9½
Seattle	91	95	14½
Hollywood	88	98	17½
Sacramento	83	103	22½
San Diego	79	107	26½

Play-offs: Los Angeles defeated San Francisco 5-0 for first place; Los Angeles 4 games, Portland 1 game; Oakland 4 games, San Francisco 1 game
Finals: Los Angeles 4 games, Oakland 1 game

Ave.	Hillis Layne, Seattle, .367
RBIs	Max West, San Diego, 124
HRs	Max West, San Diego, 43
Wins	Cliff Chambers, Los Angeles, 24
ERA	Bob Chesnes, San Francisco, 2.32

1948

	W	L	GB
Oakland	114	74	—
San Francisco	112	76	2
Los Angeles	102	86	12
Seattle	93	95	21
Portland	89	99	25
Hollywood	84	104	30
San Diego	83	105	31
Sacramento	75	113	39

Play-offs: Oakland 4 games, Los Angeles 2 games; Seattle 4 games, San Francisco 1 game
Finals: Oakland 4 games, Seattle 1 game

Ave.	Gene Woodling, San Francisco, .385
RBIs	Gus Zernial, Hollywood, 156
HRs	Jack Graham, San Diego, 48
Wins	Red Lynn, Los Angeles, 19
ERA	Con Dempsey, San Francisco, 2.10

1949

	W	L	GB
Hollywood	109	78	—
Oakland	104	83	5
Sacramento	102	85	7
San Diego	96	92	13½
Seattle	95	93	14½
Portland	85	102	24
San Francisco	84	103	25
Los Angeles	74	113	35

Play-offs: Hollywood 4 games, Sacramento 1 game;
San Diego 4 games, Oakland 3 games
Finals: Hollywood 4 games, San Diego 2 games

Ave.	Artie Wilson, San Diego/Oakland, .348
RBIs	Max West, San Diego, 166
HRs	Max West, San Diego, 48
Wins	Harold Saltzman, Portland, 23
	Guy Fletcher, Seattle, 23
	George Woods, Hollywood, 23
ERA	Willard Ramsdell, Hollywood, 2.60

1950

	W	L	GB
Oakland	118	82	—
San Diego	114	86	4
Hollywood	104	96	14
Portland	101	99	17
San Francisco	100	100	18
Seattle	96	104	22
Los Angeles	86	114	32
Sacramento	81	119	37

Ave.	Frank Baumholtz, Los Angeles, .379
RBIs	Harry Simpson, San Diego, 156
HRs	Francis Kelleher, Hollywood, 40
Wins	Jim Wilson, Seattle, 24
ERA	Jack Salveson, Hollywood, 2.84

1951

	W	L	GB
Seattle	99	68	—
Hollywood	93	74	6
Los Angeles	86	81	13
Portland	83	85	16½
Oakland	80	88	19½
San Diego	79	88	20
Sacramento	75	92	24
San Francisco	74	93	25

Play-offs: Seattle 2 games, Los Angeles 1 game;
Hollywood 2 games, Portland 0 games
Finals: Seattle 3 games, Hollywood 2 games

Ave.	Jim Rivera, Seattle, .352
RBIs	Joe Gordon, Sacramento, 136
HRs	Joe Gordon, Sacramento, 43
Wins	Marv Grissom, Seattle, 20
	William Ayers, Oakland, 20
ERA	Jim Davis, Seattle, 2.44

1952

	W	L	GB
Hollywood	109	71	—
Oakland	104	76	5
Seattle	96	84	13
Portland	92	88	17
San Diego	88	92	21
Los Angeles	87	93	22
San Francisco	78	102	31
Sacramento	66	114	43

Ave.	Bob Boyd, Seattle, .320
RBIs	Harold Gilbert, Oakland, 118
HRs	Max West, Los Angeles, 35
Wins	Johnny Lindell, Hollywood, 24
ERA	Red Adams, Portland, 2.17

1953

	W	L	GB
Hollywood	106	74	—
Seattle	98	82	8
Los Angeles	93	87	13
Portland	92	88	14
San Francisco	91	89	15
San Diego	88	92	18
Oakland	77	103	29
Sacramento	75	105	31

Ave.	Bob Dillinger, Sacramento, .366
RBIs	Dale Long, Hollywood, 116
HRs	Dale Long, Hollywood, 35
Wins	Allen Gettel, Oakland, 24
ERA	Memo Luna, San Diego, 2.67

1954

	W	L	GB
San Diego	102	67	—
Hollywood	101	68	1
Oakland	85	82	16
San Francisco	84	84	17½
Seattle	77	85	21½
Los Angeles	73	92	27
Sacramento	73	94	28
Portland	71	94	29

Play-offs: Oakland 2 games, San Diego 0 games; San Francisco 2 games, Hollywood 0 games
Finals: Oakland 3 games, San Francisco 0 games

Ave.	Harry Elliott, San Diego . 350
RBIs	Jim Marshall, Oakland, 123
HRs	Jim Marshall, Oakland, 31
Wins	Roger Bowman, Hollywood, 22
ERA	Bill Wight, San Diego, 1.93

1955

	W	L	GB
Seattle	95	77	—
San Diego	92	80	3
Hollywood	91	81	4
Los Angeles	91	81	4
Portland	86	86	9
San Francisco	80	92	15
Oakland	77	95	18
Sacramento	76	96	19

Ave.	Milton Smith, San Diego, .338
RBIs	Earl Rapp, San Diego, 133
HRs	Steve Bilko, Los Angeles, 37
Wins	Red Munger, Hollywood, 23
ERA	Red Munger, Hollywood, 1.85

1956

	W	L	GB
Los Angeles	107	61	—
Seattle	91	77	16
Portland	86	82	21
Hollywood	85	83	22
Sacramento	84	84	23
San Francisco	77	88	28½
San Diego	72	96	35
Vancouver	67	98	38½

Ave.	Steve Bilko, Los Angeles, .360
RBIs	Steve Bilko, Los Angeles, 164
HRs	Steve Bilko, Los Angeles, 55
Wins	Rene Valdes, Portland, 22
ERA	Elmer Singleton, Seattle, 2.55

1957

	W	L	GB
San Francisco	101	67	—
Vancouver	97	70	3½
Hollywood	94	74	7
San Diego	89	79	12
Seattle	87	80	13½
Los Angeles	80	88	21
Sacramento	63	105	38
Portland	60	108	41

Ave.	Ken Aspromonte, San Francisco, .334
RBIs	Steve Bilko, Los Angeles, 140
HRs	Steve Bilko, Los Angeles, 56
Wins	Leo Kiely, San Francisco, 21
ERA	Morrie Martin, Vancouver, 1.90

1958

	W	L	GB
Phoenix	89	65	—
San Diego	84	69	4½
Vancouver	79	73	9
Portland	78	76	11
Salt Lake City	77	77	12
Sacramento	71	83	18
Spokane	68	85	20½
Seattle	68	86	21

Ave.	Andre Rodgers, Phoenix, .354
RBIs	James McDaniel, Salt Lake City, 100
	Dusty Rhodes, Phoenix, 100
HRs	James McDaniel, Salt Lake City, 37
Wins	Marshall Bridges, Sacramento, 16
	Art Fowler, Seattle/Spokane, 16
ERA	George Bamberger, Vancouver, 2.45

Bibliography

Primary Sources

Archives

Kennesaw Mountain Landis File, National Baseball Library, Cooperstown, N.Y.
Miscellaneous PCL players files, National Baseball Library, Cooperstown, N.Y.

Memoirs and Autobiographies

Cobb, Tyrus R., with Al Stump. *My Life in Baseball: The True Record.* Garden City,
    N.Y.: Doubleday, 1961.

Newspapers and Periodicals

Daily Alta California, 1852–82
Los Angeles *Times,* 1903–58
New York Clipper, 1870–90
Oakland *Daily News,* 1872–1900
Oakland *Tribune,* 1900–1958
Sacramento *Bee,* 1903–58
San Francisco *Chronicle,* 1878–1958
San Francisco *Morning Call,* 1880–1900
Spalding's Official Baseball Guide, 1880–1920
The Sporting News, 1910–60
Wilkes' Spirit of the Times, 1865–85

Secondary Sources

Books

Adelman, Melvin L. *A Sporting Time: New York City and the Rise of Modern
    Athletics, 1820–70.* Urbana: University of Illinois Press, 1986.
Alexander, Charles. *John McGraw.* New York: Penguin, 1988.
Asinof, Eliot. *Eight Men Out: The Black Sox and the 1919 World Series.* New York:
    Holt, Rinehart and Winston, 1963.
The Baseball Encyclopedia. 8th ed. Ed. dir. Rick Wolff. New York: Macmillan,
    1990.
Benson, Michael. *Ballparks of North America: A Comprehensive Historical Reference
    to Baseball Grounds, Yards, and Stadiums, 1845 to the Present.* Jefferson, N.C.:
    McFarland, 1989.
Beverage, Richard E. *The Angels: Los Angeles in the Pacific Coast League,
    1919–1957.* Placentia, Calif.: Deacon Press, 1981.
———. *The Hollywood Stars: Baseball in Movieland, 1926–1957.* Placentia, Calif.:
    Deacon Press, 1984.

Blake, Mike. *The Minor Leagues: A Celebration of the Little Show.* New York: Wynwood Press, 1991.

Crepeau, Richard C. *Baseball: America's Diamond Mind, 1919–1941.* Orlando: University of Central Florida Press, 1980.

De Gregorio, George. *Joe DiMaggio.* New York: Stein and Day, 1981.

The Encyclopedia of Minor League Baseball: The Official Record of Minor League Baseball. Ed. Lloyd Johnson and Miles Wolff. Durham, N.C.: Baseball America, 1993.

Fite, Gilbert C., and Jim E. Reese. *An Economic History of the United States.* 3d ed. Boston: Houghton-Mifflin, 1973.

Gibson, Arrell Morgan. *The West in the Life of the Nation.* Lexington, Mass.: D. C. Heath, 1976.

Goldstein, Richard. *Spartan Seasons: How Baseball Survived the Second World War.* New York: Macmillan, 1980.

Hentsell, Bruce. *Sunshine and Wealth: Los Angeles in the Twenties and Thirties.* San Francisco: Chronicle Books, 1984.

Issel, William, and Robert W. Cherney. *San Francisco, 1865–1932: Politics, Power, and Urban Development.* Berkeley: University of California Press, 1986.

James, Bill. *The Bill James Historical Baseball Abstract.* New York: Villard, 1986.

Kuklick, Bruce. *To Everything a Season: Shibe Park and Urban Philadelphia, 1909–1976.* Princeton: Princeton University Press, 1991.

Lange, Fred. *History of Baseball in California and Pacific Coast Leagues, 1847–1938: Memories and Musings of an Old-Time Baseball Player.* San Francisco: n.p., 1938.

Lingeman, Richard R. *Don't You Know There's a War On? The American Home Front, 1941–1945.* New York: Putnam's, 1970.

Lotchin, Roger W. *San Francisco, 1846-1856: From Hamlet to City.* New York: Oxford University Press, 1974.

Lowry, Phillip J. *Green Cathedrals.* New York: Addison-Wesley, 1992.

Malone, Michael, and Richard W. Etulain. *The American West: A Twentieth-Century History.* Lincoln: University of Nebraska Press, 1989.

Obojski, Robert. *Bush League: A History of Minor League Baseball.* New York: Macmillan, 1975.

Okkonen, Marc. *The Federal League of 1914–1915: Baseball's Third Major League.* Garret Park, Md.: Society for American Baseball Research, 1989.

O'Neal, Bill. *The Pacific Coast League, 1903–1988.* Austin, Tex.: Eakin Press, 1990.

Pepe, Phil. *Billyball.* New York: Doubleday and Co., 1987.

Polakoff, Keith Ian, et al. *Generations of Americans: A History of the United States.* New York: St. Martin's Press, 1976.

Riess, Steven A. *Touching Base: Professional Baseball and American Culture in the Progressive Era.* Westport, Conn.: Greenwood Press, 1980.

Ritter, Lawrence. *The Glory of Their Times.* Rev. ed. New York: Morrow, 1984.

Rolle, Andrew F. *California: A History.* New York: Crowell, 1967.

Seymour, Harold. *Baseball: The Early Years.* New York: Oxford University Press, 1960.

———. *Baseball: The Golden Age.* New York: Oxford University Press, 1971.

———. *Baseball: The People's Game.* New York: Oxford University Press, 1990.

Shatzkin, Mike, ed. *The Ballplayers.* New York: William Morrow, 1990.

Society for American Baseball Research. *Minor League Baseball Stars.* 3 vols. Manhattan, Kans.: Ag Press, 1978, 1984,1985.

Spalding, John E. *Always on Sunday: The California Baseball League, 1886 to 1915.* Manhattan, Kans.: Ag Press, 1992.

Starr, Kevin. *Americans and the California Dream, 1850–1915.* New York: Oxford University Press, 1973.

———. *Inventing the Dream: California through the Progressive Era.* New York: Oxford University Press, 1985.

Sullivan, Neil J. *The Dodgers Move West.* New York: Oxford University Press, 1987.

———. *The Minors.* New York: St. Martin's Press, 1990.

Tygiel, Jules. *Baseball's Great Experiment: Jackie Robinson and His Legacy.* New York: Oxford University Press, 1983.

Voigt, David. *American Baseball: From the Gentleman's Sport to the Commissioner System.* Norman: University of Oklahoma Press, 1966.

Whittingham, Richard, comp. and ed. *The DiMaggio Albums.* New York: Putnam's, 1989.

Zimbalist, Andrew. *Baseball and Billions: A Probing Look inside the Big Business of Our National Pastime.* New York: Basic Books, 1992.

Zingg, Paul J. *Harry Hooper: An American Baseball Life.* Urbana: University of Illinois Press, 1993.

———, ed. *The Sporting Image: Readings in American Sport History.* Lanham, Md.: University Press of America, 1988.

Articles and Book Chapters

Anderson, Rick. "P.C.L. Expects to Survive Loss of Seattle, San Diego," *Baseball Digest* 27, no. 4 (May 1968).

Barney, Robert K. "Of Rails and Red Stockings: Episodes in the Expansion of the National Pastime in the American West," *Journal of the West* 17, no. 3 (July 1978).

Brown, Warren W. "A Few Innings from the Coast League," *Baseball Magazine* 24, no. 3 (February 1920).

Carino, Peter. "'The Ballparks Are Like Cathedrals': Stadia in American Culture," *NINE: A Journal of Baseball History and Social Policy Perspectives* 1, no. 1 (Fall 1992).

Claire, Fred. "Make Way for the Coast League," *Baseball Magazine* 91, no. 4 (July 1955).

Conlin, Bill. "Crisis in the Coast League," *Baseball Digest* 13, no. 2 (March 1954).

Connors, Kevin. "I'll Stick with the Coast League," *Sport Magazine* 12, no. 6 (July 1952).

Cooper, Tony. "Breaking the PCL Color Barrier," San Francisco *Chronicle*, March 1, 1993.

———. "West's Short-Lived Black League," San Francisco *Chronicle*, March 3, 1993.

Daniels, Stephen M. "The Hollywood Stars," *Baseball Research Journal* 9 (1980).

Felber, Bill. "The Changing Game," in John Thorn and Pete Palmer, eds., *Total Baseball.* New York: Warner, 1989.

Franks, Joel. "The California League of 1886–1893: The Last Refuge of Disorganized Baseball," *The Californians* 6 (May-June 1988).

———. "Of Heroes and Boors: Early Bay-Area Baseball," *Baseball Research Journal* 16 (1987).

———. "Organizing California Baseball, 1859–1893," *Baseball History* 4 (1991).

———. "Sweeney of San Francisco: A Local Boy Makes Good, Then Not So Good," *Baseball History* 2, no. 4 (Winter 1987–88).

Gregory, L. H. "P.C.L. Majors in Managers," *Baseball Digest* 10, no. 5 (May 1951).

Hall, Stephen S. "Scandals and Controversies," in John Thorn and Pete Palmer, eds., *Total Baseball*. New York: Warner, 1989.

Halsinger, H. G. "Here's P.C.L.'s Side," *Baseball Digest* 7, no. 5 (May 1948).

Hoie, Bob. "The Minor Leagues," in John Thorn and Pete Palmer, eds., *Total Baseball*. New York: Warner, 1989.

Hudson, Mary Ann. "It Was Much More Than Minor Pastime," *Los Angeles Times,* October 19, 1990.

Lotchin, Roger W. "The Darwinian City: The Politics of Urbanization in San Francisco between the World Wars," *Pacific Historical Review* (August 1979).

Martin, Al H. "The Pacific Coast League," *Baseball Magazine* 3, no. 5 (September 1909).

Nemec, David. "A History of Baseball in the San Francisco Bay Area," *San Francisco Giants Official 1985 Yearbook*. San Francisco: Woodford Associates, 1985.

Norris, Frank. "San Diego Baseball: The Early Years," *The Journal of San Diego History* 30 (Winter 1984).

Park, Roberta J. "San Franciscans at Work and at Play, 1846–1869," in Donald J. Mrozek, ed., *Sport in the West*. Manhattan, Kans.: Sunflower University Press, 1983.

Salsinger, H. G. "Here's P.C.L.'s Side," *Baseball Digest* 7, no. 5 (May 1948).

Schroeder, Bill. "The 1934 Los Angeles Angels," *Baseball Research Journal* 6 (1977).

Stern, Joseph S., Sr. "The Team That Couldn't Be Beat: The Red Stockings of 1869," *Cincinnati Historical Society Bulletin* 27 (1969).

Stump, Al. "The Final Innings," *Los Angeles Magazine* (1990).

Svanevik, Michael, and Shirley Burgett, "The City's Long Tradition as a Baseball Town," *The Times,* February 28, 1992.

Tomlinson, Gerald. "A Minor League Legend: Buzz Arlett, the 'Mightiest Oak'," *Baseball Research Journal* 17 (1988).

Tuttle, W. C. "Baseball's Great Minor Circuits," *Baseball Magazine* 55, no. 2 (January 1937).

Tygiel, Jules. "Pioneers of the Pacific Coast League," *The Museum of California Magazine* 13, no. 3 (November-December 1989).

Voigt, David. "America's First Red Scare—The Cincinnati Red Stockings of 1869," *Ohio History* 73 (1969).

Watson, Emmett. "The Coast League Is Full of Characters," *Sport Magazine* 16, no. 7 (July 1954).

Wolf, Al. "Coast Deal a Long Way Off," *Baseball Digest* 6, no. 8 (October 1947).

———. "Coast League's No Ghost League!" *Baseball Digest* 15, no. 1 (January-February 1956).

Zingg, Paul J. "The Phoenix at Fenway: The 1915 World Series and the Collegiate Connection to the Major Leagues," *Journal of Sports History* 17 (Spring 1990).

Index